SENSEI SELF DEVELOPMENT SERIES

Collection of Books 1-5

1. Your Attitude of Gratitude
2. Procrastinating Procrastination
3. Restoring Restorative Rest
4. Money Machine
5. Fine Margins of Mental Health

Sensei Paul David

COPYRIGHT PAGE

Sensei Self Development Series: Collection of Books 1-5,

by Sensei Paul David,
Copyright © Year 2021.

All rights reserved.

978-1-990106-54-5 SSD Collection of Books 1-5 Paperback

978-1-990106-53-8 SSD Collection of Books 1-5 Electronic book

This book is not authorized for free distribution copying.

www.senseipublishing.com

@senseipublishing
#senseipublishing

Check Out Another Book in This Series Visit:

www.amazon.com/author/senseipauldavid

Or

Search Amazon.com #senseipublishing

Get Our FREE Books Today!

Click & Share The Links Below

FREE Kids Books
lifeofbailey.senseipublishing.com
kidsonearth.senseipublishing.com

FREE Self-Development Book For Every Family
senseiselfdevelopment.senseipublishing.com

Join Our Publishing Journey!

If you would like to receive FUTURE FREE BOOKS, and get to know us better, please click www.senseipublishing.com and join our newsletter by entering your email address in the pop-up box.

Follow Our Blog: senseipauldavid.ca

Follow/Like/Subscribe: Facebook, Instagram, YouTube: @senseipublishing

Scan the QR Code with your phone or tablet

to follow us on social media: Like / Subscribe / Follow

Thank You from The Author: Sensei Paul David

Before we dive in, I'd like to thank you for picking up this book. Your time is valuable, and I know there are many other similar books out there, but you chose to invest in mine, and that means everything to me.

Now that you're here, and if you stick with me, I promise to make our time together valuable and worthwhile.

In the pages ahead, you will find some areas of information and practices more helpful than others - and that's great because as you apply what works best for you. You will benefit from an exciting transformation of character and knowledge. Enjoy!

Your Attitude of Gratitude

Develop Simple Gratitude Skills for Better Living

Sensei Paul David

YOUR ATTITUDE OF GRATITUDE

Develop Simple Gratitude Skills for Better Living

Sensei Paul David

CONTENTS

Welcome 1

Breaking Down Negativity 8

Highlighting Gratitude 17

Challenge #1: The 7-Day Negativity Diet 27

Challenge #2: 30-Day Gratitude Round-Up 33

New Skills, New Habits, New Beginning 39

Today is Looking Good 45

References 47

Thank You

Before we dive in, I'd like to thank you for picking up this book. Your time is valuable, and I know there are many other similar books and courses out there that offer to help, but you chose to invest in mine and that means everything to me.

Now that you're here, and if you stick with me, I promise to make our time together valuable and worthwhile.

In the pages ahead, you will find some areas of information and practices more helpful than others - and that's great because as you apply what works best for you, you will benefit from an exciting transformation of character. Enjoy!

Welcome

"Let us rise up and be thankful, for if we didn't learn a lot today, at least we learned a little."
— Gautama Buddha

The word gratitude is a beautiful word for us to include in our lives and daily practices. It is derived from the Latin word *gratus*, which means "thankful, pleasing." Therefore, in its simplest expression to be grateful is to have an appreciation and express thankfulness. In my case, I am grateful that you have chosen to read this book. However, more than my gratitude to you should be your thankfulness to your own curiosity about this book's contents and how it may guide you in a meaningful way.

The journey of discovery is shared with you is one not everyone will attempt. Your interest sets you apart and through the process of improving one's self, nurturing and self-care naturally exist. Whether you walk away with a little or a lot, you will walk away with a changed perspective for the better.

You will grow a bit more aware, gaining an understanding of the skills to help you in all areas of your life.

Perhaps you'll begin to enjoy and appreciate newfound curiosity to go beyond the surface level of life. You'll grow willing to dive into what really crafts your life—your internal perspective on all matters, both from within and in the world around you. There is no better way to recognize some of life's most precious things, large and small, than from your attitude of gratitude.

Yes, the attitude of gratitude is a common expression, easily found today in many resources. Despite its popularity, my experiences have revealed a few people experience the bliss that comes with authentic gratitude. The primary reason for this is a lack of focus. It doesn't appear to be present in many people so they can see wonderful things for what they are worth... In each moment and with a present state of mind.

It is so easy to get distracted. There is a chance that as you read this warm welcome to you, your thoughts drifted off a time or two. This has become so common to many people that it is considered human nature. Such does not have to be the case; our human nature is what we make it out to be, which means we can make it one of focus and inward serenity. The world's chaos you may feel does not have to be at home within you.

Chaos often stems from negativity, which leads to heaviness; heavy thoughts and challenges focusing on the right things. Have you ever noticed this in your life? Most have. My ambitious, yet worthy aspiration, is to help you move past the negative and dense thoughts and toward what is brighter and lighter. When your attitude and gratitude work together, you will experience this.

With an attitude of gratitude, you are continually challenging yourself to bring joy into your reality.

This is important to you for many reasons. A few that may be of interest to you include

- more balanced perspectives of situations in your life;
- stronger personal relationships;
- recognition of positive forces in your

life;
- less stress;
- and better emotional and physical wellness.

The study conducted for the Greater Goods Science Center for John Templeton University and titled The Science of Gratitude[2] also notes how gratitude can vary depending on age, gender, and even nationality. Expressions of gratitude were also impactful when it came to recovery from certain mental and physical disorders. The benefits mentioned are worth your investment of time so you can gain an understanding of your starting point. This is where I come in and want to help. So, come as you are into this journey and know that if attention span and focus are your challenges, what is being shared is done so with you in mind.

This is what you will need as you go through the pages of this book:

- Curiosity: you want to learn more about how you can tap into an attitude of gratitude that serves you well in life. The bonus is how a better you can be

of service to others.
- A compelling purpose to follow through: by having something in specific to inspire you to use this information to spark change, you will be more connected with your "why" in taking on the ideas, information, and challenges in this book. Some examples of compelling purposes are
    - children and grandchildren;
    - spouses and friends;
    - career goals and ambitions;
    - a need for better emotional health;
    - a need for better physical health;
    - a recharge of a life that feels dull and weighed down.

You are never too old or too young to discover the beauty of gratitude in your life. In fact, in a research paper listed on the NCBI website titled *Preschool-aged children's understanding of gratitude: Relations with emotion and mental state knowledge1, it states:* "Children with a better early understanding of emotions and mental states understand more about gratitude." This is a reminder of how habits we develop as a child can carry us into adulthood without us being fully aware of it. As an adult, you can act to change this. Better yet, you can help children be connected to gratitude from their earliest formative years.

- A calendar (paper or phone): in order to monitor and track changes, a calendar is required. All of us have heard how "time flies by." We must also remember sentiments such as what psychologist Philip Zimbardo says: "Time matters because we are finite because time is the medium in which we live our lives."
- A notebook: taking notes of what stands out to you in this book is going to be relevant to how you track your progress. Rather than think, where was that again, write it down. This will also help to reinforce what stands out to you and incorporate a stronger memory recognition. Hand to paper is a powerful way to develop new habits.

This opportunity should feel exciting, promising. Remembering how it is designed to help you grow with short and effective exercises helps take the pressure off. If you commit to the time to start, you will find it easy to follow through all the way to the end. Congratulations on starting this and enjoy the process.

Sensei Paul

Breaking Down Negativity

"I will not let anyone walk through my mind with their dirty feet."
— Mahatma Gandhi

Negativity is a powerful force to deal with. Once it becomes dominant it grows even stronger. Addressing it, in whatever form it may come to you, is important. It appears to us through:

- negative people around us, and,

- our own thoughts.

We are all able to shield ourselves from negative external forces while evicting that negativity we feel due to our own thoughts and actions.

In this chapter, negativity will be broken down so you can discover all the ways it currently impacts your life. There is a chance you've never taken the time to evaluate this before, which makes this information exciting, necessary, and perhaps a bit startling. Please remember, be gentle with yourself and understand why knowing is the starting point to change.

NEGATIVE BARRIERS

It may catch you off guard to acknowledge how negativity holds you back from the very things you want most in life. It works as a repellent for good and positive energy. Shifting away from this can only be beneficial to you.

Amy Morin, a clinical social worker, wrote an article for Psychology Today online titled *6 Bad Habits that Will Sabotage Your Success*[1]. In this article, she talks about putting yourself down and states: *"It's impossible to perform well when you're telling yourself 'You're stupid' or 'You can't ever do anything right.' Negative self-talk will discourage you from putting in your best effort and it will drag you down fast."*
Morin's advice on how to handle this: *"Stop the put-downs:* Talk to yourself like a trusted friend. If you wouldn't use such harsh words with someone else, don't allow your inner critic to say them to you."

A good chain effect happens when you stop being negative to yourself through your thoughts and actions. You create a boundary where you become less tolerant of others' negativity, thereby lessening it.

NEGATIVITY VERSUS ACHIEVEMENT

Whether a person has negative tendencies or not, they usually notice negativity in others. Here are some examples of how this internal dialogue or real-time conversation may sound like.

- I hope <insert name> doesn't come to the party. All they ever do is complain about <insert topic>.
- <Insert name> is so cranky. They must be a nightmare to work with.
- No matter what happens, I am going to avoid <insert name> as much as possible.

Have you ever heard one of these statements or a variation of one? Have you ever said something similar? These negative thoughts surface when we want to protect ourselves from those who overwhelm us with the way they communicate and presumably feel.

And when you are a person such as this, you are going to have thoughts comparable to these examples:

- I'll never get the job. They always pass me over.
- What's the point in saving up money? Some crazy and unexpected expense always comes up.
- I'm just destined to be alone.

Statements like what is listed here are all indicators of a life glitch that involves negative thinking. Thankfully, glitches can be fixed.

NEGATIVELY INFLUENCED RELATIONSHIPS

Relationships are the essence of life. They define our experiences, whether we are alone or with others. Negativity is one of the biggest influencers of the outcome of any relationship we have in our lives, both personal and professional.

Hiroko Akiyama et al. wrote a paper for The Journals of Gerontology titled *Negative*

Interactions in Close Relationships Across the Lifespan[2]. In this paper, it is noted: "Close relationships can be positive and negative. They provide people with joy, comfort, and support. At the same time, they can be a source of conflict, frustration, and disappointment."

Akiyama further states: *"The literature suggests three plausible explanations for decreasing negativity in close relationships: maturity, familiarity, and contact frequency. The first explanation suggests that with increasing age people mature. They acquire social skills from experience, learn to control their emotions, and improve their emotional understanding."*

What makes this study particularly interesting is that more positive relationships seem to exist in people who learned to develop good relationships prior to the inundation of technologies such as social media. Yes, social media gets picked on much of the time but there are links to show its impact on negativity and relationships that cannot be ignored.

When you think of your life, think of how nice it would be to live by—and show others—how to thrive in positive relationships. This is a life-shifting change that creates a ripple of positivity.

THE STRESS FACTOR

If you desire to manage your stress, you will need to create a mix of habits and thought patterns geared toward stress management. This means you need to build up

- resilience,
- gratitude,
- and focus.

In addition, you need to evaluate your environment in its entirety, including personal habits, friends, and family. Do you spend free time indulging in the negative instead of accentuating the positive? Determine this and you may find the source of stress.

Also, the type of work you do can impact stress. Some pleasing news is that even if you find your work unrewarding, there is a way to be at peace with it and still feel the impact of positive thoughts in a work environment, more than negative responses.

The key to all this working for you is to commit to releasing anxieties and stressors when they do not help you live in a more positive manner.

PERSONAL INVENTORY

With all the access to the information we have, it is easy to want to evaluate ourselves. This is not always beneficial but when it comes to personal habits—such as negativity's influence in our life—self-evaluation is required. Embrace this process.

Every one of us has negative habits in our lives. The ones who don't allow themselves to get blocked by these habits are the ones who put steps in place to keep them in check.

It's time to put some thought into the negative habits you may have. If you are reading this from a book, you can feel free to write in the spaces below. Or, just like the digital book holders will do, use a notebook to write down all the steps you are taking as you work on this worthwhile task.

The negative habits impacting me most are:

1. _____
2. _____
3. _____
4. _____
5. _____
6. _____

Upon reflection, how does it make you feel when you use your negative habits on yourself and others, both intentionally and unintentionally?

_____
_____
_____
_____
_____

STATEMENT OF UNDERSTANDING

For our purposes, the statement of understanding for all the exercises in this book is a simple sentence or two to relay what you have learned and what you hope to adjust in your behavior to better connect with an attitude of gratitude.

Here's an example of a statement of understanding that applies to this chapter:
I am disheartened that I don't have a meaningful intimate relationship in my life, enough so that when I see someone else happy I go out of my way to cast negative thoughts toward them. This has an undesirable impact on me and I am ready to change this.

Now, you write down your statement of understanding about one or more of your negative thought patterns/habits. This will help you become aware of what may be worthy of you to work toward.

_____

_____

Highlighting Gratitude

"We need to learn to want what we have, not to have what we want, in order to get stable and steady happiness."
— The Dalai Lama

One of the most beautiful things to hear, speak, and feel is a sentiment of gratitude. Positive feelings emit from this experience that can often carry a person through their entire day with more grace and dignity. Why would you choose to not seek out feeling this way daily, or at least as much as possible?

GRATITUDE'S HELPING HAND

This is something, author unknown, found on an online meme. It is a wonderful example of how gratitude is a helping hand for all of us in our day when we invite it in.

You've got to start romanticizing your life.

See your commute to work as cute and fun.

Make every cup of coffee you've ever had the best one you've ever had. Make small, mundane things exciting and new.

When you do these things you truly start living;

you look forward to every day.

With gratitude, you will find you achieve more because you are mentally aligning yourself with

- better physical and psychological health;
- more empathy and less aggression;
- increased mental strength (resilience);
- and better sleep.

Most challenges people face come amidst a poor night's rest. In the article by Linda Wasmer Andrews titled *How Gratitude Helps You Sleep at Night*[1], found at Psychology Today online, she shares this research:

"Psychologists Robert Emmons and Michael McCullough asked people with

neuromuscular disorders to make nightly lists of things for which they were grateful. After three weeks, participants reported getting longer, more refreshing sleep.

"Following up on this lead, researchers at the University of Manchester in England looked at how gratitude might affect people's snooze time. Their study included over 400 adults of all ages—40% with sleep disorders—who completed questionnaires that asked about gratitude, sleep, and pre-sleep thoughts. Gratitude was related to having more positive thoughts, and fewer negative ones, at bedtime. This, in turn, was associated with dozing off faster and sleeping longer and better.

"In short, when you cultivate gratitude throughout the day, you're more likely to have positive thoughts as you're drifting off to sleep. Rather than ruminating over the friend who forgot to call, you're thinking of the coworker who stayed late to help you. Instead of obsessing over bills, you're thinking of the new client you just landed. With positive thoughts as a lullaby, you're more likely to drift off into a peaceful slumber."

Health, stress, happiness, and achievement all have common threads between them which link gratitude to wellness. The two challenges you'll be doing in this book will work directly with this. The exciting thing is, they can be used effectively and in an age appropriate way, incorporating your entire family (and even workplace) into making positivity the habit of choice.

THE ROLE OF GRATITUDE IN OUR RELATIONSHIPS

Gratitude plays a valuable role in cultivating and maintaining peoples' relationships, in all areas of their lives. According to a paper presented by The Greater Good Science Center at UC Berkeley[2], regarding intimate relationships:

"Receiving a thoughtful benefit from a partner was followed by increased feelings of gratitude and indebtedness. While men in the couple reported more mixed emotions than did women, experiencing more gratitude from these acts of kindness predicted both partners feeling more connected and satisfied with their relationship the next day."

Additionally, noted in this same paper:

"A subsequent study asked some participants to express gratitude more frequently to a friend or romantic partner; other participants were asked to focus on their daily activities, increase their grateful thoughts about their partner, or focus on positive memories that included their partner. The researchers found that, compared to the other participants, those who expressed more gratitude toward a romantic partner or close friend at one time point reported greater comfort in voicing relationship concerns in the future, and that expressing gratitude more often led to more positive perceptions of a friend, which in turn led the participants to be more comfortable voicing relationship concerns. These findings might have therapeutic implications, as they suggest that expressing more gratitude to a partner or friend may nurture other skills that help improve relationships, such as making people feel more comfortable discussing potential relationship conflicts."

Through finding better ways to use gratitude in our intimate relationships, we are also learning valuable skills to

take out into the world and connect positively with all life relationships.

STRESS "LESS"

Just as negativity can elevate stress, gratitude can reduce it. When we remember all the things there are to appreciate in this world, it becomes significantly easier to savor the small things and keep a "reality check" of our lives that are rooted in goodness. Life becomes less focused on what may possibly go wrong and more appreciative of all that is good.

A nice way to help manage stress is to think about lessening it one day at a time. We can only manage what we are given in a day, which makes it quite logical to choose to dwell on what we are grateful for over what we are concerned about. This doesn't mean we don't address concerns and problems. It refers to spending time on our stressful problems from the healthier mental perspective that comes with gratitude.

GRATITUDE'S RIPPLE EFFECT

The carryover effects of gratitude are easy to correlate to sentiments from people who volunteer their time: they feel the rewards of what they've contributed as much as those who received their time and attention benefit. How incredible!

What we do to improve our own lives has the potential to have a profound and positive impact on another's life too.

Dr. Martin E. P. Seligman is a psychologist at the University of Pennsylvania. He tested the impact of various positive psychology interventions on 411 people, each compared with a control assignment of writing about early memories. This was one of their assignments, as noted in a Harvard Health Publishing study for Harvard Medical School[3]: *"When their week's assignment was to write and personally deliver a letter of gratitude to someone who had never been properly thanked for his or her kindness, participants immediately exhibited a huge increase in happiness scores. This impact was greater than that from any other intervention, with benefits lasting for a month."*

Take a few minutes and imagine how you might change a life by doing something similar. This is a wonderful, simple-to-do activity that even the smallest child can participate in. Perhaps they draw a picture for someone they are grateful for instead of writing a letter.

PERSONAL INVENTORY

Robert Brault penned: "Enjoy the little things, for one day you may look back and realize they were the big things." This sentiment states the intent of this personal inventory exercise. It is meant to be an enjoyable process for you to dive into what you may be grateful for in your life, from small to large. You'll want to focus on the habits you have in expressing these things, evaluating if you show gratitude

- automatically,
- with heart,
- at certain times of day,
- to create a favorable shift to your mood,
- or in other ways not mentioned here.

If you don't have many of these habits currently feel free to write down when you see yourself using gratitude. You know more about an attitude of gratitude now than you may have just a short time ago.

My gratitude habits are:

1. _____
2. _____
3. _____
4. _____
5. _____
6. _____

Upon reflection, I am aware of how I use gratitude habits in my daily life. This is how these habits impact me and others, both intentionally and unintentionally.

_____
_____
_____
_____
_____
_____

STATEMENT OF UNDERSTANDING

It's time to connect personal meaning to the information you've learned about gratitude habits. Here is an example of how a statement of understanding for this chapter may look:

One of my most cherished times of day happens right away in the morning when I wake up. As I stretch and welcome the day, I think of all my blessings, including my comfy pillow and even the gentle breathing of those I love who are still sound asleep.

_____
_____
_____
_____
_____

Your warm and appreciative thought is one you can use to keep you centered and focused on gratitude's importance.

Challenge #1: The 7-Day Negativity Diet

"Negativity is cannibalistic. The more you feed it, the bigger and stronger it grows."
— Bobby Darnell

A negativity diet will leave you feeling fuller and more satisfied than you've possibly felt in a long while. And like most diets, it'll be easy for the first day, then there will be a few tough days, and then it will grow easier again. Only, in our case, instead of craving food, it's resisting negative thoughts.

Our brains are tricky. They constantly bombard us with negative thoughts. Why? Mostly because we've let them get away with doing that to us for a long time. So, like a stubborn person, the brain resists change until we wear it down.

The eventual result of a negativity diet is that positivity takes over, and that is

exactly what you want your brain to respond to.

HOW THE 7-DAY NEGATIVITY DIET WORKS

This is one of the easiest diets to understand—which gives you something to be grateful for immediately.
Everything you do this week is going to focus on one thing: eliminating negative thoughts. This includes

- in what you say,
- in what you do,
- and in how you act.

If a negative thought surfaces, you will be prepared to safeguard yourself against it by

- interrupting your attention,
- keeping your mouth shut,
- and relaying a grateful thought.

You can do these things!

Making It Past the Negativity Hunger Pains

The action you will take if you're craving a taste of negativity will include discovering the: 1) how; 2) why; and 3) when.

1. *How*

    How did you get to this negative moment? Perhaps it was a trigger from something another person said or an event that happened to you. Take some time to think of how the negativity crept in right away so you can stop it from creeping in further.

2. *Why*

    Why would you be compelled to spend your energy on this negative thought? There are few (if any) examples of when spending extensive time dwelling in negativity has produced anything positive. Contrary, when using positive means to deal with what's negative, you can dissolve or solve situations and not carry their heavy weight in your being.

3. When

When does negativity seem to sneak up on you? Depending on your personality, this could happen at a typical time like it does for most people (hungry, tired, stressed, etc.) or it could happen at unexpected times (ex: your kid smarting off to you, a fight with your spouse, someone cutting you off in traffic). It's up to you to step up to your defense and know when it's happening so you can counteract negativity right away.

By following through with your 7-Day Negativity Diet, you are going to feel so much better—mentally and emotionally lighter. Once you feel this way, it's a place of betterment you'll want to remain in touch with.

Your Diet Details

Now it's time to write down your plans so you can be prepared to go on a healthy mental diet to clean out negativity.

- Write down the date you want to start your 7-Day Negativity Diet: _____

- Write down the date it will be in 7 days:
  _____

- Write down how you will go about being steadfast in your negativity diet:
  _____
  _____
  _____
  _____
  _____

- If you struggle with your 7-Day Negativity Diet and fail at first, are you willing to start over?
  _____
  _____
  _____

(If your answer isn't "yes," find a way to commit to a "yes.")

STATEMENT OF UNDERSTANDING

I will benefit from this 7-Day Negativity Diet most by

_____
_____
_____
_____
_____
_____

Challenge #2: 30-Day Gratitude Round-Up

"Feeling gratitude and not expressing it is like wrapping a present and not giving it." — William Arthur Ward

If this challenge was a billboard, it would be a simple one: 30 Days to Your Attitude of Gratitude.

HOW THE 30-DAY GRATITUDE ROUND-UP WORKS

The results of this challenge are fantastic, and it is very easy to do. All you need is either you or another person, and a minute of your time committed to the round-up every day, for 30 days.
Here is what you are going to do:
1. Ask yourself or someone else what they are grateful for. Do this in the morning so you can carry the spirit of gratitude around with you.

2. Write down what you or the person is grateful for in your notebook. See the beauty in appreciating the moment. Smile and breathe in as you absorb the positive thought.
3. Review this at least once every 10 days. Mark it down on your phone if you need to. When doing the review, take time to appreciate the variety of things you or others are thankful for.

Please note, with this exercise, you are encouraged to incorporate others into it, although it is not required. The reason this is a good idea is that you can already begin to spread the idea of gratitude to someone else, which is a reinforcement for you. Additionally, in turn, others may keep gratitude's positive energy moving in their own lives, and in others.

It's Round-Up Time

A common setback people have about incorporating others into the 30-Day Gratitude Round-Up is that they feel awkward asking others what they are grateful for. This is understandable and will feel uncomfortable the first few times you do it if you've never done it before. If this is you, remember these things to help assure you that all is well:

- Sometimes people struggle more when they try to find an answer within themselves than they do asking someone else.
- People like opportunities to talk about what's nice in their lives. Some people, believe it or not, feel it is bragging to express gratitude so they keep these thoughts to themselves. However, expressing gratitude isn't bragging because every person in this world has something to be grateful for and they can set an example for someone else on how gratitude works.

> **TIP: If you come across a person who shrugs or cannot give you a sincere answer, just smile and move on.**

Here are a few people you may want to consider asking about what they are grateful for:

- Spouse or partner
- Children
- Co-worker
- Random person (if you're brave—maybe coffee house line)
- Your driver (bus, Uber, Lyft, etc.)
- Postal person
- Cashier

Everyone is somebody you can ask if you feel comfortable doing so. An interesting observation that has been noted is many people find the opportunities to ask about gratitude start to come naturally—without a second thought—as they incorporate it into their day. Are you the next person to recognize this?

REALIZING YOUR BENEFITS

A few of the benefits of this exercise have already been laid out in this book. One example would be making gratitude a positive habit in your day. This is the goal in the end; to recognize all that you can to be grateful for, even in your life's crazier moments.

Additionally, after 30 days is up, you are going to feel other positive side effects, including:

- Enthusiasm to evaluate gratitude every morning
- Ideas on how to further incorporate gratitude throughout your day
- More smiles because you have much to be grateful for
- A better outlook on life
- More energy to draw the attention of the right kinds of conversations, opportunities, and people
- Less stress and tension
- An openness to find creative solutions to make other types of changes in your life

This challenge is a win/win. What's also exciting about it is how it's an easy habit to get kids into early on. Imagine this:

> Your small child is in the cart in the grocery store line and the cashier's scanning through your purchases.

Your child asks the cashier: "What are you grateful for today?" The cashier is surprised and then smiles. Maybe answering something like: "Meeting such a nice kid like you."

Do you think that the cashier would share what happened with someone else? They likely would, because it felt good and it's memorable — rare (although hopefully becoming more commonplace).

STATEMENT OF UNDERSTANDING

I am excited to benefit from my 30-Day Gratitude Round-Up by

_____

_____

_____

_____

New Skills, New Habits, New Beginning

"Depending on what they are, our habits will either make us or break us. We become what we repeatedly do." — Sean Covey

The commitment to develop new skills and habits can be challenging in many cases. Mostly because the rewards are not always immediate. With establishing an attitude of gratitude that lasts, you have an edge because it

- doesn't take a lot of time,
- it's not complex,
- and you feel internal rewards rather quickly.

With most habit development, the reward seems to be the key to its success. With poor habits, the rewards can be immediate (smoking or comfort food, for example). Good habits sometimes take longer—practicing gratitude being an exception.

Please accept the wonderful opportunity you have here for what it is. Take advantage of the wisdom and steps to a new beginning that is being shared next. Enjoy the process.

3 Nuggets of Wisdom to Guide You

Creating a new skill or habit doesn't come instantly. Although simple and ideal for those who are lacking focus, even creating an attitude of gratitude will require a commitment from you. Allow these 3 nuggets of wisdom to guide you.

1. Acknowledge that human nature naturally does what it must do, not what it should do. This means that we are often in survival mode, only thinking of an immediate result over a long-term benefit. Therefore, a commitment is needed to look beyond the "immediate" and into the betterment of your future.
2. Recognize a habit can take a bit of time to form. This happens for several reasons, including how challenging

the habit is the amount of effort you put into the change and the mindset and frame of experiences you have in the beginning. All people are different in the amount of time it takes to develop a habit or new skill. Your calling is to focus on your growth—it's not a race against others.

3. Set up a calendar for your attitude of gratitude commitment for at least 6 months. This will give you ample time to act, reflect, and recognize the benefits you are receiving. This is the inspiration that can keep you going until the habit is formed. It's also worth noting that inspiration is different than motivation. Motivation typically lasts about a day. Inspiration has the potential to last a lifetime.

By following these nuggets of wisdom you'll find yourself being more diligent and kinder to yourself. There is no downside to this!

3 Steps to a New Beginning

Take the time to reflect on the possibilities of what could exist with a stronger presence of gratitude in your life. Make a difference by making a commitment to these 3 steps.

1. Think of everything you stand to lose over the next years if you do not make a shift in your mindset to one of positivity and gratitude. Ask yourself these questions:

    a. Do I feel the goodness of life today?

    b. How do I help others feel gratitude and appreciation?

    c. Would I want to hang around me for a day if I just met myself, as is?

2. Create a clear picture of what your life is like with more gratitude in it. Ask yourself these questions:

    a. How do I desire to feel when I wake up in the morning?

    b. What does it feel like to give or receive a genuine smile of gratitude?

    c. What benefits will I receive from practicing gratitude consistently?

3. Make your commitment and "seal the deal" by stating this out loud: "I am a grateful person." Do this in the present tense each day to remind yourself. There is no limit on how often you can do this, either. Whatever it takes is yours for the taking. Think of how much a musician practices to master their instrument. This also requires practice and it is achievable by all. What makes you special for doing this is your commitment to it, as not everyone has it.

These 3 steps will get you going; the way you feel will keep you flowing into your attitude of gratitude.

> **TIP:** This is an invitation to meditation to help you make shifts to your mindset. Feel free to take advantage of the guided meditation practices I've created for you by visiting or downloading the app: 'Insight Timer' and searching for or clicking this link <u>Sensei Paul David</u>. You'll find a variety of meditations, both for adults and with a focus on children.

STATEMENT OF UNDERSTANDING

My attitude of gratitude is worth my commitment because:

_____
_____
_____
_____

Today is Looking Good

"I am tomorrow, or some future day, what I establish today. I am today what I established yesterday or some previous day."
— James Joyce

May you feel as excited about this life opportunity for yourself as I feel for you. You're on the cusp of making a transition for the better. You've gained an understanding of information about:

- The consequences in your life caused by negativity
- Ways that gratitude can enhance your life, as well as the lives of those around you
- An exciting vision of how gratitude can play out in your life
- Practical steps and strategies to help you create the habits and skills it takes to gain your attitude of gratitude

To help you learn how to accomplish an authentic, now-a-part-of-you, gratitude practice, you can implement the challenges laid out for you.

- Challenge #1: The 7-Day Negativity Diet
- Challenge #2: The 30-Day Gratitude Round-Up

You've also learned why you want to have an attitude of gratitude. Because of this, you know that it is a pursuit worth remaining on for as long as you need.

It's a great day to be alive! And I thank you for your commitment to gratitude and a better approach to all you partake in.

References

Invitation: if you are interested to dive deeper into any of the information shared, here are the resources where details were found.

INTRODUCTION

[1] Jackie A. Nelson, et al., Preschool-aged children's understanding of gratitude: Relations with emotion and mental state knowledge, March 28, 2012, extracted from:
https://www.ncbi.nlm.nih.gov/pmc/articles/PMC5224866/
on January 6, 2020.

[2] Summer Allen, Ph.D., The Science of Gratitude: A white paper prepared for the John Templeton Foundation by the Greater Good Science Center at UC Berkeley, May 2018, extracted from:
https://ggsc.berkeley.edu/images/uploads/GGSC-JTF_White_Paper-Gratitude-FINAL.pdf
on January 20, 2020.

Breaking Down Negativity

[1] Amy Morin, 6 Bad Habits that Will Sabotage Your Success, Psychology Today online, March 3, 2016, extracted from: https://www.psychologytoday.com/us/blog/what-mentally-strong-people-dont-do/201603/6-bad-habits-will-sabotage-your-success on January 6, 2020.

[2] Hiroko Akiyama et al, Negative Interactions in Close Relationships Across the Lifespan, The Journals of Gerontology, *Series B*, Volume 58, Issue 2, March 2003, Pages P70–P79, extracted from: https://academic.oup.com/psychsocgerontology/article/58/2/P70/557810 on January 6, 2020.

Highlighting Gratitude

[1] Linda Wasmer Andrews, How Gratitude Helps You Sleep at Night, Psychology Today online, November 9, 2011, extracted from:

https://www.psychologytoday.com/us/blog/minding-the-body/201111/how-gratitude-helps-you-sleep-night extracted on January 6, 2020.

[2] Summer Allen, Ph.D., The Science of Gratitude: A white paper prepared for the John Templeton Foundation by the Greater Good Science Center at UC Berkeley, May 2018, extracted from: https://ggsc.berkeley.edu/images/uploads/GGSC-JTF_White_Paper-Gratitude-FINAL.pdf on January 6, 2020.

[3] In Praise of Gratitude, Harvard Mental Health Letter, June 5, 2019, Harvard Health Publishing: Harvard Medical School, extracted from: https://www.health.harvard.edu/mind-and-mood/in-praise-of-gratitude on January 6, 2020.

PROCRASTINATING PROCRASTINATION

Proven Strategies to Crush Habits of Delay & Indecision for Life!

Sensei Paul David

CONTENTS

FOREWARD 57

CHAPTER ONE INVESTIGATING THE ORIGINS OF PROCRASTINATION 63

    Is Procrastination a product of nature or nurture? 63
    Insights into Procrastination 65
        Investigating how you Think 65
        Boredom 67
        Fear of Failure 67
        Fear of Expectations 68
        A Carefree Attitude 68

CHAPTER TWO PROCRASTINATING PROCRASTINATION 70

    How to Procrastinate Procrastination 71

CHAPTER THREE THE TRIGGERS OF PROCRASTINATION AND TIPS TO AVOID THE RESPONSE 82

CHAPTER FOUR REASONS FOR YOUR LACK OF MOTIVATION 94

CHAPTER FIVE FLIPPING PROCRASTINATION TO ACTION 103

CHAPTER SIX THE FINAL 20 WAYS TO OVERCOME PROCRASTINATION 111

INDEX: 119

Foreward

In the modern world, writing a book is no longer as challenging as it used to be. Therefore, many authors are putting out works by the day across the globe. Nonetheless, many so-called self-help materials out there do not offer value to the readers. Many only end up increasing the knowledge of the readers without adding practical steps that can give the readers a new lease of life. The good news is that this book is not one of such materials.

It is a practical guide based on the rich experience, astuteness, and expertise of the author. He is renowned for his uncanny ability to help people by simplifying seemingly complex concepts like chunking into short & easy to understand ideas. He is also adept at converting uncertainty into curiosity to form habits of continuous self-education. In 2002, he entered the corporate world and was introduced to having bigger responsibilities apart from his work.

That was when he started realizing that he needed to review his procrastination protocols. Before then, he was fond of doing things the hard way by starting with the biggest tasks. This approach led to frustration and delay in refocusing. He often struggled to take new actions because of the fear of failing. However, he was able to turn his life around. How? He realized that an early start leads to an early finish. He found out that a simple mental shift in notion could make a tremendous difference.

Things started getting better when he started taking massive actions with the maxim, "Early Start, Early finish." He started asking more questions, and he realized that he has been achieving improved results with almost anything he chooses to do. The idea of living life without delays started getting clearer, and he has drastically reduced wasting time when acting on an idea. He is more courageous to take action, believing that an early start will lead to an early finish.

Over the years, many people see him as the proponent of the adage "Early Start, Early Finish." Many individuals have also enjoyed success by adopting this maxim. Therefore, he has decided to come up with a comprehensive material that explains this procrastination-conquering mindset. This effort is what has given birth to this project. What do you stand to gain by reading this guide?

This book offers you a streamlined synopsis and solution strategies in one place. It also provides a path to action. This simple resource guide makes timely coaching available to you whenever you need it each step of the way and as often as you like. It is written in plain English with FREE specialized bonus guided meditation. Therefore, you will be able to access a recap of the finer points of the book faster and easier than ever before.

Thank You from The Author: Sensei Paul David

Before we dive in, I'd like to thank you for picking up this book. Your time is valuable, and I know there are many other similar books and courses out there that offer to help, but you chose to invest in mine, and that means everything to me.

Now that you're here, and if you stick with me, I promise to make our time together valuable and worthwhile.

In the pages ahead, you will find some areas of information and practices more helpful than others - and that's great because as you apply what works best for you. You will benefit from an exciting transformation of character and knowledge. Enjoy!

Welcome

"Don't put off until tomorrow what you can do today."

Benjamin Franklin

Procrastination has always been a problem for many people, whether you work in an office or you perform your job at home. However, the COVID-19 pandemic has sent the world into a tailspin as many have started to work remotely to stay safe and slow the spread of the deadly virus.

Nowadays, it is even easier to start procrastinating because your mind is wandering, and you are focusing on other things. You get side-tracked.

Let us explore ways to overcome your habits of delay and indecision.

Congratulations on starting this and enjoy the process.

Sensei Paul

Chapter One

Investigating the Origins of Procrastination

IS PROCRASTINATION A PRODUCT OF NATURE OR NURTURE?

This is an important question we need to answer. Indeed, procrastination is something we all do. However, some people seem to have more control over this habit than others. Could the answers be found in our genetic makeup? Placing the bulk of the fault at the feet of our parents is the easy way out for most of us.

We would claim that we are innocent because we are acting based on the training we received when we were younger. In some cases, we will look for any research out there that can prove that our bad habits are based on the way our brain was hardwired at an early age to perform the way we do as adults.

Interestingly, some studies have proven that procrastination can be traced to our genetic makeup. For example, the University of Colorado Boulder found in a study that procrastination is inherited. (1)

The above-mentioned study carried out by the University of Colorado Boulder also found the following:

- Procrastination is inheritable
- Impulsive actions and procrastination share a genetic variation
- Goal management is a part of procrastination and impulsivity

The study showed that 46 to 49 percent of people inherit procrastination and impulsivity. Therefore, genetics appears to influence how you effectively prioritize important goals and regulate your actions.

The good news is that whether you blame your procrastination on your genes, environment, or personality, it is fixable. Let us start to explore strategies and tips to help you overcome delaying things in your life and putting off until tomorrow what you should complete today.

INSIGHTS INTO PROCRASTINATION

The best method to conquer procrastination is to first understand what it is and what it is not. Listing tips and strategies that can help against this bad habit might end up being useless if we don't understand the phenomenon we are up against.

INVESTIGATING HOW YOU THINK

In this section, we will perform a simple exercise that involves answering some questions that require honesty and sincerity. This concise test will help you to have an insight into how you think.

Why do you procrastinate? Could it be because you cannot carry out a task, or are you simply not interested in doing it? This question is simple, but it is foundational to stopping this limiting behaviour. Once you answer it sincerely, you have solved half of the problem.

Are you inadequately equipped to perform the task? Naturally, you will avoid a task that you lack the skills required to perform.

For example, you will not want to go near a pool if you don't know how to swim. You will do all you can to avoid any situation that will warrant you to swim because you know that you cannot do it. In the same way, a child will procrastinate about doing homework that he does not know how to tackle. You might wrongly assume that he is lazy. However, it is better to find out if he knows how to solve the problem in the first place.

Note that it is not always the case that you procrastinate because you cannot accomplish a task. There are also situations where you delay carrying out activity because you don't feel like doing it. For example, if you choose to delay mowing the grass of your house because it is sunny, it is not about a lack of ability, but you are just deciding not to do it.

You need to be able to identify your motive for delaying a task. The first step you need to take to conquer procrastination is to be able to know when you are choosing to avoid a task because you don't possess the skills to do it and when you just lack the enthusiasm to get it done.

BOREDOM

The world is full of exciting toys that can distract you from doing what you need to do. In some cases, you prefer to play games or see a movie rather than do something productive with your time. One of the reasons you do this is because you don't find that task interesting. If a task makes you <u>feel bored</u>, then you are going to avoid it.

FEAR OF FAILURE

The fear of failure is one of the most common reasons people procrastinate. No one wants to do something without getting a positive outcome. Therefore, it is natural that you avoid a task when you feel you are not likely to succeed in it. Fear of failure emerges at a young age.

When kids are fearful of the mockery of their peers, they often resort to avoidance. For example, they might delay participation in a sports competition because they don't feel they can succeed. Unfortunately, this fear continues into adulthood for many people. So, you need to recognize your fears and learn to tackle them to stop procrastinating.

Fear of Expectations

It sounds weird, but the reality is that some people are also afraid of success. They have enjoyed so much success in their lives that they become a victim of the expectations that comes with their previous success. When you achieve a lot, people tend to forget that you are human. They put so much pressure on you to always succeed. If you are not careful, you will start avoiding some tasks because you don't want to ruin the reputation you have built before now.

Many people who were superstars when they were young have ended tragically because of unmanaged expectations. Some of them ended up being drug addicts because they could not cope with the pressure. So, just like the fear of failure, you also need to watch out for fear of success.

A Carefree Attitude

A carefree and nonchalant attitude will lead to laziness. Meanwhile, when you are lazy, you will procrastinate a lot. Laziness will affect your relationship because it will make you lose the trust of your loved ones. For example, your spouse might hire a helping hand to carry out chores because you make excuses for not doing them.

So, the earlier you destroy this harmful habit, the better for you. No one will want to trust you to handle anything significant when they cannot trust you to give it your best. Your skills and expertise will not be able to save you if you are not hardworking. Many will soon discover that you are not worth their trust due to your laziness.

Chapter Two

Procrastinating Procrastination

A double negative can have a multiplier effect to produce something positive, and that can be the case when it comes to procrastination. We have discussed the reasons people procrastinate. So, you are ready to learn how you can start tackling this bad habit. Indeed, you can reduce the rate at which you delay what you need to do. From this section and beyond, you will be exposed to tips and strategies for overcoming procrastination. Take your time to read through each one and select the ones that work for you.

How to Procrastinate Procrastination

You can counter the tendency to procrastinate in your life by leveraging the following tips:

Plan for Tomorrow

You must plan for the next day. You will waste time when you wake up in a day, and you don't have things you need to do already. Planning and analyzing will waste time and end up wasting part of your peak period. So, take five minutes every day to plan for the next day.

Stick to the Plan

You need to have a plan and stick with it, especially when things get tougher. Note that challenges are parts and parcels of life. So, don't be perturbed when things are not going your way. Successful people rarely procrastinate because they have a plan, and they will stick with it. Changing your plans will make you waste time devising new strategies for the new goals.

Measure your Self-Esteem

It is better to be overconfident than have low self-esteem. When you are self-confident, you will approach every task with assurance, which cuts out procrastination. However, when you have low self-esteem, you will not be confident of succeeding in a task. As a result of that, you will not want to attempt. Even when you choose to carry out the activity, you will not put in your best because you are not sure that things will go your way.

Avoid Distractions

One of the things that lead to procrastination is when you are not focused. It is easier to be caught up in the web of digital devices in today's tech-savvy world. Many people cannot stop looking at their phones while working or carrying out a task. Such people will end up spending more than usual to do what they need to do. In some cases, you will have to postpone a task because you have wasted too much time on frivolities.

Learn Until the End

You should ensure that you keep learning. It is normally,I like an old dog learning a new trick when you engage yourself in a task that is not familiar. However, if you have the right attitude, you can learn how to do anything. Once you keep your focus to learn from the beginning to the end, you will reduce the tendency to procrastinate.

Give yourself Incentives

Psychologists have done a lot of work on how incentives increase behaviour while punishment reduces it. If you have ever trained a dog, you will notice that it will perform an act more frequently when you reward it for doing it. In the same way, you can train yourself to inculcate the right habits by rewarding your good behaviours. For example, promise to have a nice treat when you perform a task within a specified period. The incentive will help you to keep working hard towards the goal. Over time, you might not need to reward yourself again because of the feeling of accomplishment after achieving a feat, by itself, is enough motivation to avoid procrastination.

Forgive Yourself

Interestingly, it is often easier to forgive others than forgive yourself. Unfortunately, you will only get stuck in the same position when you refuse to release yourself from the past hurt. Research has proven that you will reduce the rate of procrastination when you practice self-forgiveness. This is since you will create a more positive outlook of yourself when you let go of past mistakes. (2)

Be Accountable

You should have the discipline to focus on what you need to do and get it done. However, it can be challenging to supervise yourself. If you are finding it difficult to concentrate and do what you need to do on time, you should consider asking a loved one to check on you. You likely focus on what you need to do and achieve it when you have someone who will find out about your progress rate. Besides, there are online tools such as the Procrastinator, which can help you to be proactive and self-monitor your time.

Act Fast

According to Benjamin Franklin, "Don't put off until tomorrow what you can do today." These words say a lot about acting quickly instead of wasting time. You need to act fast. What do you have to lose when you choose to start now? So, start now!

Limit Distractions

It is almost impossible to avoid distractions in the modern world. We all want to avoid being left behind. Besides, you have juicy discussions on social media you want to read every day. Nonetheless, you must find a way to limit your distractions to achieve your targets personally and in other areas of your life.

Conquer Negative Self-Talk

The voices in your head are louder than the ones around you. Your mind is an active processor that absorbs both positive and negative stimuli around you. So, you need to stay in charge to avoid letting your mind on the loose. When you leave your mind on "auto-pilot mode," it will groom destructive thoughts that can lead to procrastination.

Empower yourself by changing the thoughts in your mind from a compulsion to choices. For example, you should not think, "I have to do this," rather, think, "I want to do this." This paradigm shift can give you a new lease of life to help you avoid delaying what you need to do.

Eat that Frog

Many people make the mistake of approaching their tasks by starting from simpler tasks. This approach can lead to not having enough energy, later on, to carry out the more challenging ones. So, it is always better to do the difficult tasks first during your peak period.

Work at Peak Periods

Your peak periods are the parts of the day when you are the most effective. It is the part of the day you can focus your energy on a job and accomplish it. Find out what works best for you and work during that time.

Leverage Time Management Tools

Indeed, the modern world is full of distractions. However, we also have many tools out there that can help you manage your time and increase your efficiency. Individuals and organizations take advantage of time management apps to boost their productivity, and you can do the same. Trello and Toggl are some of the most popular options out there.

Know when to Take a Break

Taking a break is not evil if you know how to do it at the right time. Taking a break does not always mean that you are lazy. It can boost your efficiency. When you rest a bit after working hard, it can help you to refresh and have enough energy to work harder again. You cannot achieve much when you feel jaded. You might end up procrastinating because you have lost the zeal and energy to keep working.

Get Your Blood Pumping

Many companies are going digital. Indeed, it comes with many advantages, such as working in the comfort of your home. It is also cost-effective for both companies and employees. However, it is easy to start slouching in your office chair and feel sleepy. You can start struggling to complete tasks because you have been too static while sitting for several hours in front of your computer. So, you need to take a break once in a while to get your blood pumping again. A quick workout will do the magic.

Work with a Deadline

Working with a deadline reduces the chances of procrastination. One of the reasons you waste time on a task is that you feel you have excess time to complete it. One study discovered that the ideal way to time yourself is by working for 52 minutes and then give yourself 18 minutes to relax.

If you are wasting too much time, you need to start giving yourself the deadline for your tasks. Be accountable to a person to ensure that you stick with it. (3)

Sectionalize your Work

One of the techniques to avoid mental exhaustion and procrastination is to break your work into sections. This method is crucial when the task is going to take a lot of time. You likely avoid starting a task when it is going to be very demanding. So, you should break it up into smaller bits. This technique of increasing efficiency is called **chunking**. Of course, it is just a trick of the mind. Nonetheless, it is effective for accomplishing demanding tasks.

Reinvigorate yourself with a Snack

Taking a snack can become a distraction if you are not careful. However, it is one of the best ways you can recharge without feeling tired. An apple or a banana are great foods to refuel. (4)

Work with a Friend

Your friends can inspire you to achieve your goals and accomplish your dreams. If you have a friend that has similar tasks to achieve, you can work together to inspire one another to stay focused. However, you need to know when to quit if the person ends up distracting you.

Take Advantage of Social Media

Social media has many ills to it. However, we cannot deny that it has many benefits if you learn to use it to your advantage. Many people take advantage of social media platforms to share different things, including recipes, images, and videos. You can also take advantage of the platform to share your targets with your friends and loved ones. When you tell your friends and families about your goals, you will be under pressure to ensure that you achieve them. Note that this approach may not be the best if you have many strangers as your "friends" on a platform like Facebook.

Avoid Looking for the 'Perfect Time'

Many people end up not doing what they need to do because they were waiting for the perfect time to do it. For example, you might want to wait until the weather is cooler to mow the yard. You might not have the same enthusiasm to do it by that time. Besides, you might have to attend to something crucial and urgent by then. So, once you are free to do something, do it immediately.

Reduce your Stress Levels

Stress is inevitable. However, you must learn to cope with it and manage it effectively. When your stress levels are high, you will not have the desire to do what you need to do on time. Therefore, you need to work on reducing your stress levels as much as possible. There are many ways you can achieve this. For example, you can explore to help you focus your mind and improve your mood. Gratitude does not mean that you have things going your way. Instead, it is a deliberate choice to focus on the positive aspects of your life rather than the negative parts.

So far, we have discussed some strategies and tips that can help you against procrastination. Subsequently, in the next chapter, we will dig deeper to help you have a better understanding of this subject. We will explore what leads to procrastination with a more detailed approach.

Instant <u>gratification</u> is the order of the day. The issue with this mindset is that it will prevent you from enjoying better and more significant benefits. One of the reasons we procrastinate is that what you need to do immediately does not offer any benefit at the moment. We will explore this issue and other relevant ones in the next section.

Chapter Three

The Triggers of Procrastination and Tips to Avoid the Response

We need to understand what triggers procrastination to cut out this destructive habit. According to Tim Picryl, the author of *Solving the Procrastination Puzzle:* seven triggers make us want to delay what we ought to do at the moment. (5) They include:

- Boring
- Ambiguous
- Frustrating
- Unstructured
- Lacking in personal meaning
- Difficult
- Not intrinsically rewarding

Nonetheless, many activities are in these categories. To carry out such tasks, you will have to mentally rename them to a different label, among other solutions to ensure that you do what you need to do. The tips in this chapter will help you arrest the slide.

Keep a Journal

Amazingly, keeping a journal has many benefits, including the improvement of mental health. Therefore, it is not surprising that many people are leveraging this concept to improve their efficiency and avoid procrastination. When you are writing, your mind is involved. So, the process creates an emotional connection to the things you are writing, thereby giving you the motivation to act on them. This technique is particularly important to the goal-setting process. You can also use journaling to practice gratitude. It involves writing things that make you happy in your life in your journal. If you have this culture, you will have more reasons to keep going during tough times and will avoid wasting time.

Emotional Connection

You cannot carry out a task enthusiastically when you are not emotionally connected to it. So, you need something that can make you have positive feelings while doing the activity. There are many ways you can achieve this. If the task will fetch you some money, think about all the nice things you can do with the money once you complete the job. Besides, if it is something that will enhance your career, think about all the perks that come with it such as the paycheck and respect.

Resist the Urge

The statement that emotions are antithetical to logic could not have been more correct. Our emotions are part of what makes life beautiful. However, they can be serious drawbacks that can make you procrastinate. So, do not give in to your emotions that are telling you to procrastinate. Instead, let your logic take control. In order words, focus more on the reasons you should work rather than check your social media app. The natural urge is to do things that are not stressful. However, you have to choose to be logical rather than emotional.

Redefine the Triggers

It is not good enough to know the triggers. It is also vital that you redefine them when performing a task to overcome procrastination. You can use the template below to do yours.

Example:
- Difficult = Demanding
- Boring = Misunderstood
- Ambiguous = Needs to be solved
- Frustrating = Requires skills
- Unstructured = In Progress
- Lacking in personal meaning = Needing relevance
- Not intrinsically rewarding = Delayed significant reward

Renaming tasks in this format sounds simple. However, it has tremendous impacts. By seeing a difficult task as challenging, you will push yourself to get the needed resources to succeed at it. You will look forward to the sense of achievement you will get after completing the task. In the same way, treat a seemingly boring task as misunderstood. One of the reasons we feel an activity is not exciting is that we don't understand how to go about it. You can turn things around by asking questions from other people who are more adept at carrying out the task.

Know Your Resistance Level

Your resistance level is your breaking point. Once you get to that point, you will not want to perform any task. For example, you might struggle if you spend an hour reading and you want to spend the next hour preparing a report. This struggle shows that you have reached your resistance level. Once you get to that point, you will start getting frustrated. Therefore, you need to take a break. You should consider breaking a demanding task into segments to avoid getting exhausted. For example, you can spend thirty minutes on a part and move to the next one after ten minutes break.

Be in Charge

Many books and articles have been written on the power of the mind. Indeed, the mind is a powerful thing. The way you train it can make or mar you. Your mind can make you avoid some tasks if you allow it to control you. When you think about something, then it can become worse than it is in reality. Instead, you need to just force yourself to start, and you will probably be amazed to find out that it is truly not as bad as you envisioned. It might be somewhat easy once you begin to work on the project and stop procrastinating. Therefore, you need to be in charge of your thought to control your emotions.

Start with the Intention to Finish

When you don't have the plan to finish a task you have started, any point can be the end. Research has proven that you will not feel at ease when you are yet to complete a project. So, the trick is to start first to finish. When you are determined to finish the work, you are most likely going to start immediately and push until the end. (6) Even if you did not manage to complete the task, you would have done enough to complete the rest as soon as possible.

Think about how much Money Procrastination will Cost you

When you think of the fact that delaying a project will make you lose money, you will be under pressure to get the job done at once. One of the ways you can inspire yourself is to think about how much you will earn when you are done with the work. This approach is particularly effective when what you are procrastinating about has financial gains to it. This simple formula can make you treat your projects with more urgency to get them done on time.

Impact relationships

The last thing you want is to lose the trust and affection of your loved ones. Indeed, family and friends are supposed to overlook your imperfections and still love you and support you. Nonetheless, you need to make it easier for them to do so. No one will hand over trust to you. You have to earn it through your actions.

Your friends and families will avoid trusting you with responsibilities when you have a knack for wasting time and giving excuses. They will rather look for someone that will not disappoint them. Procrastination can also affect your relationship with your spouse. It can lead to arguments, especially when you are not repentant and penitent. So, consider the effects time-wasting can have on your relationships to encourage you to make amends.

Envision Your Success

Think about what you stand to gain when you complete a task and let it inspire you to avoid delays. Experts call this approach a form of reverse engineering. It involves standing on the podium first and working from there to get to where you are. Keeping your eyes on the prize is a fantastic motivation technique that can inspire you to avoid putting off whatever you need to do now.

Lack of Purpose

Naturally, you will not commit to an activity when it does not make sense to you. For example, you cannot enjoy a game when you don't know its essence. If you see football as just a stupid game where people are shooting a ball into goalposts, you will not participate in the sport. One of the reasons you procrastinate is that you cannot see any reason you should carry out a task.

If it is something new to you, endeavour to ask questions from the right people so that you can have more insights into why it should be done. Until you find a reason to carry out an activity, you can never be enthusiastic to do it. So, you need to do some soul-searching until you find a common ground. Many online and face-to-face programs can help you search for meaning in life. Leverage them to give yourself a boost and overcome procrastination.

Sense of Impeccability

Your background and previous experiences can make you a perfectionist. Perhaps, you were an "A" student in school, and you will never accept anything less than that. Indeed, there is nothing wrong with having an excellent academic record. Generally, you should want to be the best in whatever you are doing. However, life does not always give you what you want or even deserve. So, you need to avoid an obsession with perfection. Failure to do so will make you waste time and lose opportunities to start small. You can't always have a perfect score. So, you need to learn to take the positives and keep pushing rather than waiting for perfect opportunities to act.

Fear

It is okay to be afraid once in a while. We all have reasons to fear. So, you should not feel like a weakling when you are scared. However, it is a problem when you allow your fear to crush your confidence, making you procrastinate. Sometimes, the reason you are afraid is due to your past failures. Nonetheless, you have to forge ahead. You should learn from your past failures rather than make them reasons you cannot try again. You can turn your life around if only you are willing to do so. If you notice that you are often anxious and fearful, you should talk to a counsellor to help you with therapy. Nonetheless, the most effective therapy is self-determination to try again after failing.

Truth Avoidance

Misinformation has a great impact on a person's psychology. The University of Michigan carried out a study to validate this claim. The result showed that misinformation influence how you think. Interestingly, you might not even realize it. In some cases, these wrong beliefs will form your worldview and make you do the wrong things. You might even be subconsciously avoiding the truth and procrastinating so that you can stay in your comfort zone. So, you will have to take deliberate steps to liberate your mind to absorb the truth. This form of procrastination sounds strange but it is real. For some people, it is a survival mechanism for avoiding difficult situations. At the height of it, you will have to see a counsellor before you can reverse the effects of this self-imposed delusion. (7)

Avoiding Demanding Tasks

One of the reasons people procrastinate is the avoidance of tasks they deem challenging and demanding. Thinking about how difficult a task is can drain your energy and reduce your mental strength to cope with it. In some cases, you will keep wasting time because you don't want to start. However, in some situations, you will start with smaller tasks first. It is still a form of procrastination because you might be too tired and mentally exhausted to tackle the demanding task when you are done with the easier tasks. So, your best bet is to face your fears and do the difficult tasks first.

Low Motivation

Motivation is the fuel that powers every activity. Motivation is linked to your energy levels. When you are fatigued, you will not want to do anything. You might need to rest and eat to be ready again. Nonetheless, physical strength does not mean that you will have the desire to get something done. If you are physically sick, talk to your doctor on time because that will affect the urgency with which you carry out a task. In the same way, if you are mentally exhausted, you need to act fast. If it is a recurrent issue, you should consider speaking to a mental health expert.

Lack of Clarity

You cannot be at your best if you lack direction. It is when you know what to do that you will know the direction to direct your energy and other resources. So, you will delay doing something when you are not sure about what you need to do. Don't hesitate to ask questions when you find yourself in a situation where you are confused. Asking questions will help you to have better insights into the task, thereby making you start working rather than delay what to do next.

Chapter Four

Reasons for your Lack of Motivation

If you don't know the reason you are acting in a particular way, you cannot stop that habit. For example, if you have issues with your temper, you need to find out the sources of your irritation and frustration to turn a new leaf. In the same way, you need to be able to find out why you lack the desire to carry out a particular task to be inspired to do and complete it.

Note that you cannot succeed in any endeavour if you don't have the zeal and passion to go all out to get it done. So, you must diagnose your lack of passion and fix it as soon as possible. Some people start to lack motivation because of something that is going on in their current life. This section will help you to discover the likely reasons you are not inspired to do something and the tips to overcome them.

Major causes of lack of motivation include:
- Stress
- Fatigue
- Depression
- Other more pressing needs
- Lack of new ideas
- An emergency
- Surrounding yourself with negative vibes
- Previous failures
- Working in a discouraging environment
- Ambiguous goals
- Global issues like a pandemic or recession

According to a study carried out by Carnegie Melon University, a lack of motivation is why many people procrastinate. Nonetheless, if an individual can connect a task with goals and intersects, the individual will feel more energized to get the work done. (8) So, seeing completing a task as crucial to your satisfaction and fulfilment can go a long way in encouraging and inspiring you to start immediately.

Goal choice and self-confidence are the two key components of motivation, according to researchcarried out by the National Academies of Sciences, Engineering, and Medicine. (9)

Setting goals gives you the direction to focus your energy. However, you cannot succeed by setting goals alone. If you don't have self-efficacy, your objectives can never be accomplished. One of the reasons you lack self-confidence is that you don't have the skills required to achieve your target.

There are many ways you can overcome a lack of motivation. The tips below are some of the most popular that has proven to be effective:

Work Environment

Your work environment is crucial to your productivity. If you are working in a place that is full of distractions, you are not likely to have an engagement with the work. Note that some distractions are "positive." For example, if you are working at home, your spouse or children may need your attention. This distraction is positive because you are also strengthening the bond of your relationship by giving your loved ones your attention. Nonetheless, it is still a form of distraction. So, it is better to be in a place where you will not have to be distracted even for the right reasons.

Ambiguous Objectives

Don't just set goals for the sake of it. Ensure you know what you want and write it down without ambiguity. For example, don't write, "I want to be the best in my career." Rather, write, "I want to make the most sales among the sales rep of my company this year." Something like this is more specific and can lead to prompt action.

Identify Your Stressors

One of the reasons you lack motivation is stress. We cannot do without stress. However, we must be able to cope with it effectively to avoid getting mentally and physically exhausted. It is easy to be emotionally drained in recent times due to the COVID-19 pandemic. The report has it that millions of people around the world have died due to sickness. Many people are worried about the virus affecting their loved ones. This situation can drive your anxiety levels very high. Nonetheless, you need to realize that your worry will not protect your loved ones.

Instead, it will only take its toll on your mental health. The best thing you can do for them is to enlighten them about the preventive measures of the virus. Don't let the situation weigh you down such that it is affecting your efficiency. If there are other reasons you are stressed and lack motivation, identify them and relieve the stress. Note that junk food or alcohol consumption should not be options for you. A workout routine and meditation are better options that can help you relieve stress without side effects.

Depression

Depression is a problem facing millions of people across the globe. This mental health condition results from stress and other factors. The advent of social media exposes many people to stressful and mentally challenging situations. Social comparison has never been easier, which leads to discontentment and lack of happiness. Many celebrities post their expensive accessories and mansions on these platforms. So, some people feel that something is wrong with them because they don't possess what those superstars possess.

Besides, some individuals have been victims of cyberbullying where many people mock them because of their body shape or other things. When you allow depression to get the best of you, you will not be motivated to work. Pay attention to the source of your depression. If it is due to your exposure to social media, you need to reduce the time you spend on those platforms. If you are still struggling to cope with depression after trying your best efforts to overcome it, see a counsellor as soon as possible.

Tiredness

Fatigue can be due to mental or physical exertion. Nonetheless, it is difficult to separate one from the other. If you are mentally exhausted, it will affect your motivation to do something. In the same way, you cannot be at your best when you are physically tired. Tiredness might mean that you are doing too much and need to slow down. If you discover that you are working too hard, you need to take a breather. You don't have to wait until you break down before you do the needful.

Priorities

When you fail to pay more attention to the things that matter to you the most, you will regret it eventually. When you are giving more time to the less relevant tasks, you will eventually lack the motivation to tackle the more crucial ones. Therefore, you must decide what your priority is and give it more time and attention.

A dearth of Fresh Ideas

When you are finding it hard to come up with new ideas, it can lead to procrastination. Writers and researchers often face this challenge. In some cases, you are just staring at your laptop screen for minutes, waiting in vain for the next idea. One of the reasons you have this mental block is that you are not working during your peak periods. If that is the case, ensure that you find out the time of the day you are at the optimum level of energy to get the job done. Also, you can reach out to friends and family to pull in fresh ideas so that you again feel inspired.

Unprecedented Events

Emergencies happen, and they can slow you down. Life is full of unprecedented situations that can ruin your plan. So, it is always good that you have another plan in case the first one does not materialize as expected. Some situations can be so shocking that they can make you lose focus and steal away all your energy or desire. However, your strength is revealed by how you react when you have to deal with an unexpected situation. Try to clear things up, accepting the fact that sometimes, things fall apart. When they do, we pick ourselves back up and refocus to get back on track.

Previous Mistakes

Your past can either mar you or make you. It all depends on you. Many people have recovered from devastating situations to get their lives on track again. Such people become a source of inspiration for other people going through tough times today. In the same way, there have been people who have had setbacks and never recovered again. No one wants to repeat their past failures. The fear of falling short is enough to make anyone drag their feet. However, you cannot let fear stand in your way. You must forge ahead to try to overcome your past shortcomings. Let your mistakes serve as lessons that will act as springboards for your future success. You can choose to give up or keep fighting. However, the latter is always the better choice.

Negative Vibes

You cannot rule out the influences of the people around you on your life. The people around you can make you lose interest in the tasks you need to do or make you delay them. Some people will tell you that you are working too hard by being focused and committed. Some honest people can say that to you to protect you from breaking down. However, some people say things like this to you so that you will not make them look lazy. Stay around the people that will encourage you to be focused and committed to what you need to do.

Chapter Five

Flipping Procrastination to Action

It takes being watchful and guidance to make children do things that do not offer them immediate gratification. They prefer playing to doing tasks such as their assignment. As we grow older, we often retain this same mindset. We still prefer to watch our favourite TV show rather than do our laundry. We know that washing our clothes will make us look tidy and clean and prevent diseases in the long run. However, watching the TV show will make us excited immediately, and the natural tendency is to choose it.

Whenever you have to do tasks with the following features, you are likely to procrastinate:

- Difficult: We all prefer to avoid tasks that are demanding and time-consuming.

- <u>Boring</u>: No one wants to be involved in an activity that is not exciting.

- Unstructured: It is tricky to focus on when a project is not systematic and procedural.

- Frustrating: When you are not making progress while learning a new skill, you can get frustrated.

- No Intrinsic Rewards: A task that does not offer positive feedback will not feel interesting to you.

- Ambiguous: When a task does not seem to be leading to a specific destination, it leads to procrastination.

- Meaningless: If you cannot decipher the essence of carrying out a task, you will not want to commit to it.

Any task that has more of the above attributes will lead to delays. You will not find enough motivation to get it done immediately.

The tips below will enable you to flip tasks that have these attributes to your advantage:

Make it Fun

There are many creative ways you can bring more life into a task that drains you physically and mentally. One of them is by buying an audiobook that you can listen to while you perform mundane chores. Find out what works for you and incorporate it into your activities. Note that you can have a collection of methods for making a chore fun. Use them randomly to avoid getting bored.

Set Aside Time

Setting a deadline often inspires prompt action, which is critical to success in every sphere of life. When you set aside time to complete a task, you will restrict yourself from losing focus. It brings a sense of urgency to what you are doing, which helps you to overcome procrastination.

Relax your Mind and Body

Your body is like a machine. Therefore, you should not be surprised that it will start malfunctioning when you abuse it. One of the ways you can avoid overusing your body is to take quick breathers. Indeed, it might seem counterproductive to do so. However, you will only end up doing more when you relax. You can rest for like fifteen minutes after rigorous labour. If you are like me, you can take a nap for twenty minutes and start again. Refreshing yourself will give you the boost to maintain your tenacity for productivity.

Reframe Your Deadline

If you are working in an organization, endeavour to seek the permission of your boss early to avoid getting sanctioned. Getting some extra hours or days can be the difference between an average job and a top-quality job. When your boss knows that the delay will increase your efficiency, it is likely he or she give you e more time, which will enable you to work with less stress and pressure. Nonetheless, ensure that you do not have a culture of asking for permission and making excuses.

Take Advantage of Melody

Music soothes the soul and can inspire you to keep going when you are feeling like stopping. Have a playlist of inspiring and melodious songs that inspires you. There are always songs that immediately make you feel better and more invigorated. Have them and use them when you need them. Note that music can become a distraction in some cases. So, you need to know when you should play songs or seek other means of motivation. In some situations, you can just play music for a while until you are inspired to focus on the task again.

Rehydrate

You will be sluggish when you don't have enough fluid in your body It is always better to rehydrate at the same time you want to take a break so that you will not have reasons to leave the job multiple times. Getting a drink should not become a distraction. So, ensure that you don't let that allow you to get stuck in other activities that can make you lose focus.

Take One Day for Hard Stuff

Take out a day of the week for doing the most demanding tasks. Of course, you need to plan. List the tasks you need to do that day so that you will not waste time on choosing the activities you need to carry out. Once you do that, the remaining activities of the week will be easier and more interesting. You will do them with less stress, and that bodes well for your mental and physical health.

Leave Your Comfort Zone

You need to leave your comfort zone to enhance your productivity. For example, being a remote worker does not mean that you have to be working at home in your pyjamas. You may choose to go somewhere you can be more focused on the task if your home is full of potential distractions. For example, if your kids often make you chat more than you should, you need to find somewhere else that ensures that you are engaged. The place might not be as comfortable as your home. However, it is fine as long as it enables you to perform at your best ability.

Avoid Frowning

The truth is that you will always have reasons to frown and be sad. However, happiness is a choice. You can choose to smile when you may be crying. Indeed, it is easier said than done. However, it is a practice that can boost your mood and help you to avoid procrastination. Your brain knows when you are smiling, and it can improve your entire disposition. If you feel happy, then you will be more willing to get things done, even if you are not truly interested in them.

Temptation Bundling

There are things you enjoy doing because they offer you pleasure such as watching your favourite TV show or playing video games. However, there are activities you would prefer not to do even though they are productive such as doing your laundry. You can integrate your temptations into your chores to make them more enjoyable. For example, you can do your laundry while listening to music.

Eliminate Unproductive Days

Little success here and there will eventually lead to something tangible. You should have a list of the things you need to achieve in a day. Always start immediately to avoid laxity and complacency. Even if you are not able to achieve everything, always ensure that you did some things to pat yourself on the back at the end of the day. If you have a zero-day, you will feel bad about yourself, and that can affect your momentum and motivation the next day.

Take Advantage of Sprints

When you have unpleasant tasks you need to complete within a short period, the temptation to postpone them is very high. However, you can inspire yourself to get to work by leveraging short sprints. Short sprints are timely frames of blocked time set aside for finishing certain tasks. For example, you can declutter your home in ten minutes by quickly picking unwanted items and disposing of them.

Chapter Six

The Final 20 Ways to Overcome Procrastination

It is hard to overcome procrastination, but it is achievable. Of course, there would not have been any need to write this book if it is not achievable. Let us look at the last ways to overcome procrastination.

The Pomodoro Technique

This technique has been around since the 1980s. It was created by Francesco Cirillo to help humankind overcome centuries of battling procrastination. The Pomodoro Technique was created after the popular kitchen timer. It involves ways to work more efficiently to make work more efficient and overcome procrastination. Cirillo realized that human beings cannot focus on two things at the same time. He also understood that people have a limited attention span. So, effectiveness could only be achieved if a person works for a condensed period and take a break before starting again. (9)

The Pomodoro Technique can be broken down into the following steps:

- Select a particular task
- Set a timer for 25 minutes
- Work for 25 minutes without distractions
- Take a five-minute break, which includes getting up and taking a walk
- Resume work for another 25 minutes
- Work for four-time blocks and then take a 15- or 30-minute break

This method aims to challenge your mind to remain focused and fresh by leveraging periodic breaks.

Leverage your Environment

You can set up your environment to inspire you to avoid delays. Students often use nudges such as photos and sayings to remind them of their goals. You can do the same thing by filling your surroundings with things that can stir positive emotions. As an adult, you can still inspire yourself by using nudges such as photos, stickers, adages, or other things that can lighten the mood and brighten your day. You can also put your awards to keep reminding you that you have what it takes to succeed again.

Choose an Overseer

Many people don't want anyone to tell them what to do. However, it is not all bad to have an overseer in your life. An experienced and calm figure who you respect can make a lot of difference. Such a person can help you to ensure that you don't lose focus.

Embrace Discomfort

Life is not a rollercoaster ride. So, expect things to be tough sometimes. Avoiding discomfort will limit how far you can go. You cannot achieve monumental success if you are willing to pay the price.

Increase your Work Gradually

If you do too much at a time, you might be discouraged to start again. Increasing your schedule steadily will enable you to train your body to adjust to new demands without breaking down.

Evaluate Impact

Evaluate things based on impact. Does the unpleasant task have a direct impact on your life? If you have answered yes, then decide to commit yourself to complete it promptly. If you need a push, then remember the impact of whatever the consequences of not taking action may be.

Use Your Strengths

Research has shown that if you use your strengths, then you will increase productivity and improve engagement. We all have strengths that enable us to set goals. So, why not rely on them? (10) When you engage in activities that do not allow you to showcase your capacity, you will look like a fish on dry land.

Watch Your Diet

One of the worst kept secrets in the world is that what you eat matters. Some food increases your energy and stabilizes your blood sugar. So, if you are feeling sluggish, such food can help you fix the situation. However, you will need to do some findings to know how to eat them in the right proportion. Note that watching your diet goes beyond simply eating a banana to boost your blood sugar level to complete one task. Rather, it involves checking your feeding habit.

If you don't eat healthy, eating one meal cannot suddenly fix all your problems. You should also find out if you have food allergies by paying attention to the way your body reacts when you consume certain foods. Some people are allergic to gluten. If that is the case for you, you will not be able to work effectively whenever you consume such food.

Some foods can spike up your blood sugar and then drain your energy. Such foods will impair your performance. They include alcohol, fried foods, fast foods, foods or drinks high in sugar, and refined carbs such as pasta or white bread.

Don't be too Comfortable

If care is not taken, comfort can make you too relaxed and procrastinate. When you are working from home, likely, you won't take your bath early in the day and even leave on your pyjamas. However, this approach might prevent you from getting in the mood to work. So, you should consider waking early, taking your bath, and dressing up to be in the mood to start working without wasting time. However, if feeling free enhances your performance, then there is no reason to change.

Reduce your Expectations

It is good to be ambitious. There is nothing wrong with setting goals and going all out to make them happen. Nonetheless, you should not think that things will always be perfect. A realistic expectation will ensure that you are not so shocked when things don't go your way such that you don't want to do anything again. (10)

Know When to Give up

You should be resilient. Nonetheless, some situations demand that you give up, and you need to be able to identify them. Don't waste time on something that will not be productive.

Practice Gratitude

Life will not always give you what you want. So, you need to learn to appreciate your success, regardless of how little it seems. When you do not appreciate what you have, you will be frustrated, and that will affect your effectiveness in your daily activities.

Be Optimistic

You need to believe the best about your future to keep working hard towards your goals. If you allow negative thoughts drain your energy, it will hamper your performance.

Be Contented

Contentment does not mean that you should be satisfied with mediocrity. Rather, it is a sense of satisfaction while working hard to achieve more. Lack of contentment will lead to frustration.

Stay Inspired

You need to stay inspired to keep going and avoid frustration. So, do all you can to keep finding reasons you need to start acting immediately.

Don't Deceive yourself

Unfortunately, many people put up appearances in the modern world. Many people like to make others see them in a way that is different from who they are in reality. When you are not honest about your progress, you will waste time unnecessarily sometimes.

Believe in the Process

Everything in life has its time and season. If you are not calm and patient, you will land yourself in trouble. Take time to meditate, relax, and breathe to achieve calmness and encourage your mind to be in the right state for work. (11)

Don't Overrate yourself

If you don't have an honest evaluation of your ability, you will end up getting stuck along the way, thereby wasting time.

Don't Hesitate to Ask Questions

Whoever is not too proud to ask questions from the right people is not likely to make mistakes. If such a person has difficulties dealing with an issue, he will be able to find answers to forge ahead on time.

Be Quick to Repent

You are not impeccable because you are a human being. So, when you make mistakes, you should be quick to admit it. When you don't repent on time, you will inhibit your progress and procrastinate.

Index:

1. Genetic Relations Among Procrastination, Impulsivity, and Goal-Management Ability: Implications for the Evolutionary Origin of Procrastination

By: Daniel E. Gustavson, Akira Miyake, John K. Hewitt, Naomi P. Friedman

First Published April 4, 2014

Volume: 25 issue: 6, page(s): 1178-1188

Article first published online: April 4, 2014; Issue published: June 1, 2014

https://www.ncbi.nlm.nih.gov/pmc/articles/PMC4185275/

2. I forgive myself, now I can study: How self-forgiveness for procrastinating can reduce future procrastination

By Michael J.A.Woh, Timothy A.Pychy, and Shannon H.Bennett of the Carleton University, Department of Psychology,

Article first published online: 26 January 2010, Available online 26 February 2010.

https://www.sciencedirect.com/science/article/pii/S0191886910000474#:~:text=As%20self%2Dforgiveness%20is%20a,encourage%20a%20change%20in%20behavior.

3. A Formula for Perfect Productivity: Work for 52 Minutes, Break for 17 Minutes

By Derek Thompson

Article first published online: 17 Septemeber, 2014

https://www.theatlantic.com/business/archive/2014/09/science-tells-you-how-many-minutes-should-you-take-a-break-for-work-17/380369/

4. Solving the Procrastination Puzzle: A Concise Guide to Strategies for Change

By Timothy A. Pychyl

Published 21 December 2013 and available at:

https://www.amazon.com/Solving-Procrastination-Puzzle-Concise-Strategies/dp/0399168125

5. A zeigarnik-like effect in the recall of anagram solutions

By Baddeley, A.

Published: 1 March 1963

https://journals.sagepub.com/doi/abs/10.1080/17470216308416553

6. New study analyzes why people are resistant to correcting misinformation, offers solutions

By Jared Wadley

Article first published online: 20 September 2012

https://news.umich.edu/new-study-analyzes-why-people-are-resistant-to-correcting-misinformation-offers-solutions/

7. Students lack interest or motivation

By Carnegie Melon University

Article first published online: 2020

https://www.cmu.edu/teaching/solveproblem/strat-lackmotivation/lackmotivation-01.html

8. Learning, Remembering, Believing, Enhancing Human Performance

Consensus Study Report

By Daniel Druckman and Robert A. Bjork,

First published: 1994

https://www.nap.edu/read/2303/chapter/1

9. The Pomodoro Technique: How to Master Your Time in 25-Minute Blocks

By Francesco Cirillo

First published online: 3 August 2020

https://www.developgoodhabits.com/pomodoro-technique/

10. Seven Signs You Are Too Much of a Perfectionist

By Walden University

Published: No recorded publishing date

https://www.waldenu.edu/online-masters-programs/ms-in-psychology/resource/seven-signs-you-are-too-much-of-a-perfectionist

RESTORING RESTORATIVE REST

PROVEN TACTICS TO REDUCE INSOMNIA WITHOUT THE GUESSWORK

Sensei Paul David

Restoring Restorative Rest

*Proven Tactics to Reduce Insomnia
Without the Guesswork*

Sensei Paul David

CONTENTS

FOREWORD.. **129**

CHAPTER ONE EXAMINING THE RESTORATION OF REST
.... **135**

    Practice Journaling... 136
    Leverage Guided Imagery.. 137
    Restorative Breathing... 141
    Resting the Body and Mind 142

CHAPTER TWO PROVEN HINTS FOR RESTORATIVE SLEEP
.... **145**

CHAPTER THREE JOURNALING YOUR EXPERIENCES .. **157**

CHAPTER FOUR FINDING EQUILIBRIUM IN ALL
    RAMIFICATIONS... **163**

CHAPTER FIVE MAKING YOUR BEDROOM A SANCTUARY
.... **172**

CHAPTER SIX MORE WAYS OF RESTORING REST **178**

CHAPTER SEVEN LEVERAGING YOGA FOR RESTORATIVE
    SLEEPS **186**

    The Link Between Yoga And Restorative Sleep 187
    Yoga Tips... 188

CHAPTER EIGHT SIGN IN AND OUT IN GRAND STYLE 191

Why You Need Restorative Sleeps And Rest 192
REM Sleep 193
Deep Sleep 194
How To Sign In And Out In Style 195
Learn The Art of Relaxation 196

INDEX **198**

FOREWORD

Sensei Paul David has always been passionate about adding value to the lives of people. He is an indefatigable researcher who will leave no stone unturned to ensure that the people around him have better experiences every day. His ability to simplify complex concepts such as mindfulness and procrastination, has always endeared him to his teeming readers all over the world. In this masterpiece, David explores how you can eliminate restlessness and restore quality sleep and rest into your life.

He has an uncanny ability to help you convert uncertainty into curiosity in order to help you form beneficial habits of continuous self-education. Apart from his training and expertise, his rich experience installs him as the best person to write this book. In 2017, he was hit by a truck and knocked unconscious while riding his bicycle. Indeed, he protected his head and center-line before impact. Nonetheless, he was left with intense back pain after surviving That started disturbing his sleep.

Just like any other person, David sought solutions to the problem. He saw a neurosurgeon who told him that he was a candidate for spinal surgery. Nonetheless, he decided not to choose that option.

He was determined to find another alternative that would help him solve the problem without surgery. He tried conventional methods, such as spinal injections and acupuncture, alongside other treatments and therapies. Unfortunately, none of them worked in the long run. Therefore, he had to learn to treat himself through some techniques he discovered.

Don't get the thinking wrong - there's no magic potion here. This book is about the strategies and techniques David learned that helped him to start sleeping like a baby again. So, if you have been suffering from insomnia, this book is for you. David knows what it feels like when every area of your life is malfunctioning because you are not getting quality sleep. That is why he has put this project together. Note that not everything in this book that will work for you.

However, you can be confident that you will find helpful tips that will improve the quality and quantity of your sleep. Reading this material offers you a streamlined synopsis and solution strategies, all in one place. It also provides you with a path to action that can coach and guide you whenever you need it. Besides, it contains a FREE specialized bonus guided meditation to recap the finer points of the book faster and easier than before.

Thank You from The Author: Sensei Paul David

Before we dive in, I'd like to thank you for picking up this book. Your time is valuable, and I know there are many other similar books and courses out there that offer to help, but you chose to invest in mine, and that means everything to me.

Now that you're here, and if you stick with me, I promise to make our time together valuable and worthwhile.

In the pages ahead, you will find some areas of information and practices more helpful than others - and that's great, because as you apply what works best for you, you will benefit from an exciting transformation of character and knowledge. Enjoy!

Welcome

"It's very important that we re-learn the art of resting and relaxing. Not only does it help prevent the onset of many illnesses that develop through chronic tension and worrying; it allows us to clear our minds, focus, and find creative solutions to problems."

Thich Nhat Hanh

Proven tips and strategies to help reduce insomnia without the guesswork

Let's start our journey by exploring the very definition of the word 'restoration'.

Restoration (noun): the action of returning something to a former owner, place, or condition, e.g. the restoration of peace.

In today's fast-paced world, it's hard to take time to rest. Everyone is overworked and stressed out. If you are like so many people, then you are a doer who is constantly striving to complete tasks in a timely fashion and still rise to the top. You probably suffer from exhaustion, burnout, and a feeling of being overwhelmed as you try to tackle everything that life throws at you. Many people don't even know how to rest because they can't shut their minds down. In this book, we will explore restoring restorative rest.

Let us explore ways to restore your restorative rest.

Congratulations on starting this and enjoy the process.

Sensei Paul

Chapter One

Examining the Restoration of Rest

Bring Tranquillity to your Body and Mind

Indeed, sleeping is a vital component of resting. Nonetheless, resting goes beyond lying down and closing your eyes. Rather, it has more to do with finding emotional balance and inner tranquillity. In fact, one of the reasons you struggle to sleep is that your mind is running from pillar to post. You cannot have quality sleep when you are mentally disturbed due to anxiety. In the same way, you cannot get enough sleep when you are drowned by thoughts of guilt and shame due to your past mistakes.

It is true that you will fall asleep if you are completely exhausted. However, that does not translate to a restful sleep. Why? Your body might shut down into a restful mode. Nonetheless, your mind will continue to race, and this can lead to nightmares. So, it is not enough to sleep for eight hours. It is all futile if you are still feeling emotionally and mentally drained when you wake up.

Therefore, you need to find a way to balance stress and relax to restore your physical and psychological health. This chapter explores tips that can help you begin this process. Here they are:

PRACTICE JOURNALING

Writing is a physical process that has a psychological impact. When you are writing, your mind is also involved. You would have noticed that many individuals have blogs where they write about different topics such as travel, dating, entrepreneurship, and many more.

Of course, there are many reasons people start a blog. Nonetheless, one of them is that it serves as a tool for stress management. Even making daily posts on social media can make you more relaxed than you can imagine. However, you don't have to start a blog to enjoy the numerous benefits of writing. Instead, you can keep a journal.

Take advantage of journaling to write your feelings, experience, goals, and strategies. This activity enables you to be more thoughtful and strategic in your approach to life. You will stop making decisions hastily, and that will improve your performance because you will start making fewer mistakes.

Leverage Guided Imagery

One of the ways you can set your mind free from entangling negative emotions is by taking advantage of guided imagery. It involves placing your mind in a particular mental setting that generates positive emotions. The positive feelings will help you create more positive energy, which ensures that you are calmer and more relaxed.

Audiotapes or scripts are used by some people for guided imagery. However, some people turn to a teacher to help them on their journey. Guided imagery helps to free the imagination to disconnect the body from destructive thoughts of the mind. According to Michigan Medicines C.S. Mott Children's Hospital, you can practice guided imagery by taking advantage of some tested and proven tips. (2) They include the following:

Sit and Take a Few Breaths

Guided imagery begins with sitting in a comfortable location. While in the sitting position, take a few deep breaths, which initiate relaxation.

Picture and Think

Thinking about a setting that inspires serenity can lead to inner tranquillity. Note that the setting you will choose depends on your personality. For example, if you are an introvert, it is not likely that you consider going to a beach as something that inspires serenity.

However, an extrovert might find peace by thinking about such a setting. An introvert is likely to find a mountain retreat peaceful. Therefore, use a setting that gives you a sense of tranquillity. Picture it in your mind and imagine finding yourself there. Think about what you will see, hear, and feel when you are there.

Choose a Suitable Pathway and Sound

If you need a path to enter guided imagery, you are not alone. Before you can choose an ideal pathway, you need to first identify what you think can give you a sense of serenity.

For example, if you consider sitting on a beach peaceful, think about the pathway that leads to the place. Go deeper into the reality of the imagination. Note that you cannot have an optimum experience if you have never had an actual experience of that setting.

I mean, you should have been to the beach before and enjoyed the inner peace that comes with sitting there. So, when you imagine being there, you will be able to easily produce similar emotions through guided imagination.

Moreover, you should pick a sound or word that is associated with the setting that gives you a sense of inner tranquillity. When you practice consistently, it will be easier for that word or sound to help you connect with the experience.

Indulge All Your Senses

To have the best experience when using guided imagery, you have to indulge all your senses. I mean, if you imagine sitting among trees, you should go beyond the sight. You should also think about the warm breeze caressing your skin. Also, imagine the sound of chirping birds.

When you are done with the guided image tour, open your eyes after counting three. If you have done it properly, you will realize that you will feel more relaxed than you were before the practice.

RESTORATIVE BREATHING

There is no life without breath. In fact, it is a subconscious activity that we don't think about unless on a few occasions, especially when we are sick. However, if you can take your time to observe your breath, it can become an interesting means of finding inner peace.

Making your breath in tune with your body can change your life tremendously and make you more aware of your surroundings.

Michigan Medicines C.S. Mott Children's Hospital developed a simple breathing exercise that helps you to gain inner peace. It involves the following steps: (1)

- Take a very deep breath
- Sustain it for awhile
- Let go as you exhale

Ordinarily, this process sounds simple. However, when you try it repeatedly, you will be surprised by the result you will get. You will experience a sense of peace and calmness that will make you want to practice the steps all over again.

Simple breathing exercises such as this helps to cope with depression and anxiety. It also increases muscle relaxation and flexibility. Therefore, it increases the quality and quantity of sleep.

RESTING THE BODY AND MIND

For many years, philosophers were at loggerheads regarding the relationship between the mind and the body. Apparently, one cannot work without the other. So, it is not good enough to rest your body. You must also work on your mind to ensure that your whole being is intact.

The good news is that it is not challenging to achieve tranquillity for both your body and mind. Despite the demands of this habit, it has enormous benefits. The tips below can make a whole lot of difference:

Have an Aromatic Warm Bath

Start by letting warm water run over your body. Then add aromatic oils or bath bombs into the water for an aromatic experience.

Enjoy Music

Listening to the pleasant tune of your favourite song while enjoying the warm bath is the perfect body and mind soothing experience. Let loose and sink into the experience as everything around you begins to come alive.

Practice Mindful Meditation

Many experts believe that meditation would have been a multi-billion dollar industry if it could've been packaged like a pharmaceutical product. This claim is not far from the truth due to the numerous benefits of practicing meditation, that has been scientifically proven.

One of the perks of this practice is that it makes people calmer and more relaxed. So practicing meditation mindfully is one of the best ways you can work on your mind and body to bring them into a tranquil state.

It involves paying attention to your breath and other things in your surroundings. You cannot have the best experiences in life when you are not present in the moment. Meditation helps you to pay attention to every detail, thereby enabling you to enjoy every moment.

Chapter Two

Proven Hints for Restorative Sleep

Despite the benefits of obtaining restorative sleep, the process is not as tricky as many people think. This chapter explores proven tips that can make a restorative sleep the norm rather than an exception in your life.

Have A Regular Sleep And Wake Time

One of the reasons restorative sleep is elusive for some people is due to their irregular sleep and wake up times. Your body needs a consistent routine that it can adapt to. When you incessantly change your bedtime and wake up time, your body will have to adjust all over again. Once your body adjusts to a rhythm, you can be sure that you will wake up more energized and reinvigorated regularly.

Rejuvenate Yourself With Sunshine

Some people don't realize how much they need sunshine. Indeed, excess of it can cause health risks. However, if you don't have sufficient exposure to sunlight, it can affect your physical and mental health. Your body needs sunshine to feel rejuvenated, thereby energizing you to complete your daily tasks. Ensure that you don't use bright light in your room when the sun sets. It can make your body stay awake and active, thereby ruining the quality and quantity of your sleep.

Don't Keep Late Nights

You will disrupt your sleep rhythm when you have a culture of sleeping late. It can be tempting to watch an exciting movie late into the night. However, it is not a healthy practice. Go to bed when you notice that it is getting late. You can always complete the movie some other time.

Moreover, you should ensure that you use your bed for sleeping in the night rather than reading or checking your social media page. Your phone's light can affect your eyes and make it difficult for you to sleep well. This habit will only ensure that you don't have a restorative sleep. You will wake up feeling fatigued and jaded.

Avoid Napping During The Day

Napping during the day is a sign that you have not been sleeping well. You should not have this habit unless during the periods when you are sick. However, you might need a nap because you are involved in a physically draining activity. In such a situation, ensure that you sleep nothing less than fifteen to twenty minutes to guarantee reinvigoration when you are awake.

Regular Exercise

The importance of regular exercise cannot be overemphasized. Note that you don't have to hit the gym to participate in exercising. A thirty to forty-five minutes routine at home can go a long way in relaxing your muscles and calming your mind. Yoga is also another option that can help you loosen your muscles to improve your sleep.

Don't Take Your Stressors To Bed

Stress is inevitable because of its importance to our lives. No one can succeed in life without going through some level of stress. You need stress in your career to push yourself to the top. You also need to put yourself under pressure to keep developing and acquiring skills.

However, a lack of stress management skills can be disastrous. For example, you should avoid taking your stressors to bed. In other words, avoid working late into the night. Let all your activities be in the day. Ensure you complete your tasks during the day and use your night for the one thing it should be used for – sleep.

Besides, unless you are a remote worker, you should avoid taking your job home. You should spend your time at home with your family and loved ones. When you allow your stress at work to affect the quality of time you spend with your family, it will eventually affect your work-life balance, which will take its toll on your mental health.

Have Bedtime Rituals

Endeavour to create a bedtime routine. This approach will make you start feeling more relaxed when that time approaches. Your body knows what is next, and it will start preparing for it. You can consider a warm bath or listen to soothing music as part of your ritual.

Just use what works for you. You should know those things that make you feel more relaxed and ready to sleep. Do them before you sleep. When you do them consistently, your body will adjust to them. In fact, one will become a trigger for the next as your muscles learn to carry out the routine.

Watch Your Diet

In case you don't realize it, foods carry chemical energy. In other words, they are chemicals that are capable of reacting with your body to cause reactions. Therefore, it is crucial that you don't take what you eat for granted. Note that what you eat includes what you drink.

Foods and drinks that contain caffeine are energizers. They work in such a way that they will keep your body active. So, it is vital that you don't take them in the evening because they will interrupt your sleep. Even if you sleep, it is likely you wake up an hour later.

In that case, it might become difficult to sleep again. You might find yourself just tossing in bed instead of sleeping. So, endeavour to drink water rather than such drinks, especially in the evening. Sacrificing your sleep will affect your activity the next day.

Reduce Alcohol Consumption

Many people use alcohol as a stress reliever. Of course, it can have short-term benefits. However, it can cause long-term health issues. So, you need to find healthy alternatives to relieve stress. However, even if you cannot do without the substance, you should avoid taking it after dinner time.

The rationale behind some people consuming alcohol after 6 pm is that it will not affect them when working or doing other daily activities. Nonetheless, taking alcohol before bedtime can disrupt your sleep. If you drink a lot, you can pass out. However, by the time you wake up, you will be feeling horrible and exhausted.

A hangover will set in, and it can make you feel useless all through the following day. It will affect your performance, especially if you are doing a job that is mentally and physically demanding. You might find yourself dozing off for most parts of the day.

Be Picky With Snacks

Yes, excess consumption of snacks can have adverse effects on your health. However, there is nothing wrong with taking snacks before bedtime. The only consideration is that you should watch the type you consume.

Choose light and bland ones to avoid repercussions. Heavy snacking can leave you waking up with heartburn or an upset stomach. On the other hand, a soothing snack will help you get the restful night sleep you desire.

Buy A New Bed

You should not hesitate to purchase anything that can improve the quality of your life. Unfortunately, many people have a culture of buying luxuries rather than necessities. A good bed is a need you cannot afford to ignore.

Note that a bed does not have to be expensive to offer you restorative sleep. Get something you can afford, that will not strain your body. This action is particularly important if your current bed is not comfortable. It is not healthy for you to wake up with back pains. Act as soon as possible.

Don't Focus On The Clock

Many individuals have the habit of watching the clock when they lay down. This is often the case, especially when the position of the clock is where you can easily see it. It is a sign of restlessness if you often check the time when you are already in bed.

If you find that you often do this, you should consider changing the position of the clock or the position of your pillow. Also, find alternative relaxation techniques that can lull you to sleep. Music can be a fantastic option.

Discard Your Worries Before Bedtime

You cannot have a restorative sleep if you are worried. There are many potential sources of anxiety in the modern world, including pressure from your job, your bills, and family issues. Social media harassment and bullying can also make you feel bad.

However, you have to avoid taking your worries to bed. Note that being anxious will not solve your problems. You should rather make plans that will help you resolve your issues. Be optimistic if you have not found one. Sleep and hope that the following day will be better.

If you think about it, you will realize that there have been many times you were worried, but you eventually wished you had not been. Many of our fears never come to fruition. So, ensure that you make realistic plans rather than worrying over what the future holds.

Work On Your Room's Temperature

Your room temperature has to be moderate for you to have restorative sleep. If your room temperature is too high, you will find yourself tossing in bed. On the other hand, if it is too cold, it can leave you waking up with a cough or catarrh.

So, it is imperative that you adjust the temperature of your room to about 70 degrees Fahrenheit or 21 degrees Celsius. According to the publication of the National Library of Medicine, sleeping in a warm bedroom for five days or more will severely impact your ability to gain a restorative rest. It also reduces sleeps time and increase wakefulness. (3)

Stay off Your Digital Devices In Bed

Many people, especially teenagers, are fond of excessive exposure to digital devices, such as computers, smartphones, and televisions. Meanwhile, this practice harms sleep. A study published by the National Center for Biotechnology Information affirms this claim. (4)

Therefore, endeavour to put down your electronics before bedtime. If you have reasons to use your phone or computer at night, wear glasses that can block out blue light.

A study published in the National Library of Medicine confirms the benefit of this safety measure. (5) You should also consider using an app, like flux, which blocks the blue light on your computer. Another option is the installation of a blue light blocker on your smartphone.

Interestingly, blue light blockers are available for both iPhones and Androids. You can even find free ones. Finally, ensure you avoid staying in front of your television for up to two hours before you go to sleep.

This approach will ensure that you enjoy a restorative sleep regularly.

Chapter Three

Journaling Your Experiences

I earlier mentioned journaling briefly. It is a crucial tool for documenting and implementing a sleep pattern that will boost your health and performance in your daily activities. Nothing significant comes by accident. So, you have to be deliberate in ending your debacle with nightmares and waking up feeling exhausted.

One of the ways you can give yourself a new lease on life is by journaling your journey. You need to document your emotions, eating habits, and sleep patterns. This approach will enable you to learn about your body, to make changes where necessary. This chapter explores tips that can make this new journey a success.

Place A Premium On The Quality Of Your Sleep

There is no doubt that quality nights of sleep have many benefits. However, many people undervalue it. Some people even associate sleeping with laziness. However, this claim is far from the truth. The only time sleeping can be seen as laziness is when you are sleeping when you ought to be working.

I have to reiterate the importance of getting a good night's rest because you can never work towards getting restorative sleep if you don't realize how essential it is to sleep well. It is when you realize that you are missing a lot by not getting enough sleep that you are ready for the next tip.

Start A Sleep Journal

Once you are convinced that getting quality sleep is not negotiable in your life, then you are ready to make the necessary changes that can restore your natural sleep pattern. One of the first things you need to do to turn the situation around is to start a sleep journal.

Documenting your experience is the best way to study your body and its sleep pattern. This technique will also help you to notice the changes happening in your body. Besides, it will help you to evaluate the impact of the sleep changes you are making, on the quality of your lifestyle.

Decide How Often You Will Update It

You should not keep a journal for the sake of it. I mean, you have to decide vital things such as how often you will update it. If not, you will be erratic in your journal entries, and that will be a complete waste of time. Don't choose a schedule that will not be feasible for you.

It is best to update your journal daily. However, if you know that you cannot be faithful to the commitment, you can take an interval of two days. Just ensure that you are consistent going forward. Note that only those that are consistent can enjoy the full benefits of journaling.

Compare And Evaluate

In case you are wondering what you need to do with the journal, I've got you. You can use it to document the impact of the tips you are learning in this book. Notice the quality of your sleep before you start practicing the hint and the changes after leveraging it.

For example, if you have decided to start winding down thirty minutes before bedtime, notice the quality of sleep you had before you made the change. Depending on the frequency at which you document your experiences, notice what has changed since.

Moreover, your journal should contain the following details:

- Your bedtime
- The duration of your sleep
- The frequency of the times you woke up in the night (if any)
- The beverages and foods you consumed during the day and before you slept
- The way you were feeling before and after

- Your stress level before and after you slept
- Any medications you took
- The regularity and routine of exercise you had
- The quality of your sleep after waking up

Be Consistent

You are not the first person to make the decision to start and keep a journal. Unfortunately, many people have journals but don't update them. It is good to start documenting your experience in a journal. However, it goes beyond that.

You have to be deliberate about staying consistent. It is when you document your experiences regularly that you can enjoy the benefits of using a journal to restore your natural sleep pattern. So, you must put measures in place to ensure that you continue the commendable art and practice of keeping a journal.

Be Accountable

One of the best ways you can ensure that you are consistent with your decision to keep a journal is to tell someone you respect about it. If you are in a romantic relationship, you can tell your partner.

This approach will ensure that you will have someone to keep tabs on you. Besides, this method also ensures that you have someone of like mind you can share your progress with. Knowing that you have someone willing to listen to your growth inspires you to continue what you have begun.

Chapter Four

Finding Equilibrium In All Ramifications

The dynamism of life demands that you find a balance. You will have to move from one phase to another, and the demands of each stage are not the same. For example, the pressure on a single person is different from that on a married person.

If you are married, and you have a job, you will have to work tirelessly to ensure that you are a responsible parent (if you have kids), an available spouse, and a reliable employee. Maintaining balance in all of these areas is essential to experiencing a restorative sleep. So, this chapter will explore how you can find balance in every area of your life to increase your chances of having reinvigorating and energizing sleep.

Take A Breather

The fast-paced nature of life can make you caught up in chasing the wind, so that you will ignore some of the most important things in your life, such as your relationships and your health. If you don't slow down sometimes, and take a breather, your health can deteriorate.

Besides, you might end up ruining your relationships because you are struggling to find time for your loved ones. The truth is that relationships die a natural death when we don't invest in them. Meanwhile, the greatest investment a relationship needs to keep growing is time. Time is crucial, especially as a parent and spouse.

You might be surprised that your partner ends up filing for a divorce because he or she feels that you don't care about him or her. So, you need to find a balance between your career and your relationships. When you have issues with your relationship, it can affect the quality of your sleep and your mental health.

Live In The Moment

You cannot enjoy life when you don't learn to live in the moment. There are a lot of beautiful things in life, but you can never focus on them when your mind is in a troubled state. The truth is that you will always have reasons to be anxious and stressed.

However, you need to learn to see beyond your troubles and fears. When you are not living in the moment, you can walk through a garden of beautiful flowers and not appreciate the beauty of nature. In the same way, you can be eating a very delicious meal but never realize it because you are anxious.

Don't let your troubles and demands of life weigh you down such that you forget to appreciate the beauty of enjoying the simple things of life. Think about your relationships and other things in your life that make you feel grateful. It is when you approach life this way that you can start getting restful night sleeps.

You need to practice meditation to see beyond the rising bills and job disappointments. Contrary to what some people think, meditation is not a practice that is exclusive to Shaolin monks. It is for anyone who wants to find inner peace and radiate calmness. There are different forms of meditation. Explore them and find the one that works for you. Regardless of the one you choose, you can be certain that your sleep will improve when you are consistent in it.

Leverage Your Strengths More

When you don't play to your strength, you will look like a flop. You have to realize that we are all wired differently. You are a unique person who has distinctive features that makes you different from other people. It is okay to have people who are your role models. However, you have to be careful about what you copy from others.

For example, some people only work best when they have to carry out a task in the early part of the day. However, some people thrive better when they have to work in the night. So, you need to discover your strength and abilities. When you do, take advantage of them.

When you work in a situation that allows you to express your abilities, you will become a star at it because of your great performance. This experience will give you a boost and will allow you to have more positive emotions. Consequently, you will have more stillness in your nights.

Be Patient

Nothing good and sustainable comes easy and fast. It often takes time and a process that cannot be eliminated. So, don't expect your body to adjust immediately to your new sleep schedule. If you have had the habit of sleeping late, your body will still expect you to continue that way.

Change things gradually and maintain consistency. Your career or responsibilities as a parent, especially a nursing mother, might have disrupted your natural sleep rhythm. You will not start sleeping early automatically. Just ensure that you are on your bed earlier than before. Your body will soon pick up the signal and will adopt the new schedule soon enough.

So, don't be frustrated if it seems as though you are not getting results from your new approach. You have to believe in the process and keep at it because it will eventually yield the results you crave.

Close Up Activities Thirty Minutes Before Bedtime

You should avoid stressing yourself before you sleep, to avoid having difficulties. It is in your best interest to wind down any task at least thirty minutes before bedtime. This approach does not mean that you should do nothing before you sleep.

Rather, take advantage of that period to take a warm bath or listen to soothing music. Checking your phone for social media updates might not be the best idea around this time due to the exposure to the blue light that comes with it. Just ensure you are in a relaxed mood before you sleep.

Sex Only

The only intense activity you can do, that will not hurt your sleep, is sex. Indeed, this activity demands a lot of energy. Nonetheless, it ends up relaxing your body to lull you to sleep.

You will be making a mistake if you do something as intense as hitting the treadmill right before you try to fall asleep. It can tense up your muscles, thereby preventing you from having a restful sleep.

Consider Sleeping Alone

I have deliberately put this tip somewhere close to the end of this chapter because it is not something you should be quick to do. It should be your last resort when you are sure that there is no other way you can go about restoring your normal sleep pattern.

However, drastic times require drastic actions. If you realize that you are struggling to sleep because your partner snores or tosses around in bed, you will have to do something about it. Sleeping with other people is often challenging. The heat from their body can make it difficult for you to sleep well, especially if your body is super sensitive.

Take time to sit with your partner and discuss the situation. Ensure that he or she is in a good mood before opening up. Besides, ensure that you and your partner did not have any issue recently, before bringing it up.

Analyze Your Habituation

Habituation refers to the process of adapting to new surroundings or a set of stimuli. For example, you might find it difficult to sleep in a noisy environment, such as a typical city, with blaring honks and barking dogs. However, you will discover that those sounds will stop being an issue in the long run.

Interestingly, it becomes an issue to sleep well again when you find yourself in more serene surroundings later. The quietness will become a problem for you. You might start getting anxious when you are not hearing sounds in the night, which affects your sleep.

If you find yourself in this situation, you might need to consider music as an alternative to the sounds you are used to hearing. It's strange to discover this. Nonetheless, the reality is that some acceptable levels of "noise" are what you need for restorative sleep.

Chapter Five

Making Your Bedroom A Sanctuary

You might never realize how much the atmosphere of our room affects your sleep until you make some changes. Your bedroom is supposed to be that place you can be where you feel safe from the troubles of the world. It ought to be a sanctuary that offers you relaxation immediately when you enter it.

However, this is not the experience of many. For some people, their bedrooms increase their stress level because of its atmosphere. In an ideal situation, your bedroom should feel cool and dark. It is in that kind of atmosphere that you can easily fall asleep and wake up refreshed.

You will struggle to have a quality sleep when you have a street light shimmering through your window, into your room. In that case, you will have to hang up light-blocking curtains to restore the needed darkness and coolness to your bedroom. According to researchers, only about 40 percent of all people wake up feeling truly rested. This data was released by YouGov Data. (6)

This section will explore various tactics that can enable you to create a relaxing and conducive atmosphere in your room. Once you get, and apply, these strategies, you will turn your bedroom into a sanctuary where restorative sleep is the order of the day.

Buy A Comfortable And Relaxing Bed

Your bed is the most important component of your bedroom. So, you must not take it for granted. The first thing you need to do to make your bedroom a sanctuary is to ensure that your bed offers you the support you need to have a restorative sleep.

The quality of your mattress also matters. A fantastic mattress will offer you optimum support on all the pressure points in your body. This support ensures that you don't wake up sore. So, don't be stingy to yourself. The essence of making money is to use it to improve the quality of our lives and others.

Therefore, you should not hesitate to buy a new bed that will offer you a relaxing and refreshing sleep you deserve. Ensure that you follow the manufacturer's instructions when taking care of it, to prevent it from sagging or experiencing wear, which does not bode well for your objective of making your bedroom a sanctuary.

Ensure You Have Comfortable Bedding

Your effort to get restorative sleep will still be futile if you get a quality bed but have low-grade bedding. You need blankets that provide warmth and pillows that offer support. When these two are missing, you cannot have the relaxing sleep you desire.

So, it is not good enough to have a comfortable bed. You should also invest in quality pillows and blankets. You need them to envelope you in your bed and give you the feeling that you are in that place where you are away from the troubles of this world.

Make Your Room More Spacious

One of the reasons some people do not feel relaxed and comfortable in their bedrooms is that they can hardly breathe in there. What I mean by this is that they have excessive items cluttering the room, making it difficult to even move around.

If your room has this description, you have to do something about it. You need to take time to declutter it. There are many techniques that can help you create space in your home by eliminating the items you don't need.

One of them is by giving away one item daily for a week. In some cases, the reason your room has too many items is that you need to relocate some of them to another place in your home. If you find out that is the case in your bedroom, move them to another room to enjoy new soothing experiences.

Leverage Essential Oils

Many people are taking advantage of aromatherapy to relax their bodies and prepare themselves to sleep like babies. Essential oils contain the ingredients that can make you unwind, relax, and drift off to sleep. So, you should consider using them to improve the quality of your sleep.

Some of the most popular options are lavender and vanilla. They help you to find yourself in an atmosphere where you will feel mentally and physically relaxed. You can consider buying them to bring in a special effect that will make you look forward to entering your room.

To make the best of the sweet smell of essential oils, use a diffuser or vaporizer to quickly dispense the smell throughout the entire room. Fill your room with this appealing scent to give it a temple ambience that will make you fall seamlessly into a restorative sleep.

Furniture Position

The arrangement of your furniture can affect the spaciousness of your room. In some cases, your room will feel too small because of the way you have arranged your furniture. So, you need to take a look at the arrangement again and make the necessary adjustments.

Look at the distance between the bed and the door. If the bed is too close to the door, you will find it difficult to walk freely. So, don't hesitate to change the position. Ideally, your bed should be far from the door.

Chapter Six

More Ways of Restoring Rest

You don't need sophisticated activities to restore your rest. In this chapter, you will find more tips that will not require radical changes to your life to restore your rest.

Use Snooze Responsibly

Before setting the alarm, think twice about it. You must be sure that you will wake up once the alarm goes off. It is crucial that you are disciplined enough to sleep for the right amount of time when you set the alarm. If you are sleeping late, then change the alarm time, if your schedule permits it.

If you leave your alarm the way it is, when you know the time set is not realistic, you will only end up hitting snooze repeatedly, which does not bode well for your aim of getting restorative sleep. The alarm will go off again, before you have barely slept enough. You will have to repeat the process again.

Therefore, it is in your best interest to set your alarm to a time you can realistically wake up to. If your alarm goes off and you feel that you need more sleep, then extend the time, rather than hitting snooze. You will only end up waking up feeling tired with that approach.

Use Earplugs

This hint is particularly important if you are living in a place where your neighbours are having wild late-night parties. You will need earplugs to reduce the volume of the noise, so that you can sleep well.

Avoid Sleeping With Pets

Many people see sleeping with their pets as a sign of love and affection for their furry friends. A study by the American Kennel

Club (AKC) shows that 45 percent of pet owners sleep with their pets. Indeed, it is a pleasurable experience for many people who do it.

However, it is counterproductive for many individuals who share the same bed with their family pet. This difficulty is due to the fact that some animals snore, toss, and turn or breathe loudly, which makes it difficult to fall asleep or stay asleep.

Besides, young puppies have a knack of waking up and doing the same to you, asking you to take them outside. Also, cats are nocturnal, and their tendency to stay awake in the early hours of the morning can affect your sleep. (7) Therefore, you should not sleep with your pet just because others are doing so. You need to be sure that the arrangement will not disturb your sleep.

Open Your Window

It is amazing to realize how much difference opening your window can make. It ensures that fresh air comes in to replace the stuffy air to give your bedroom a fresh and conducive atmosphere for restorative sleep.

Try A Leg Pillow

Most people only use pillows for their heads. However, you can make yourself more comfortable by using a leg pillow. This option is a fantastic choice, especially if you have lower back discomfort. The pain does not have to be extreme to hurt you. Slight discomfort is enough to ensure that you don't have restorative sleep.

So, you can make life easier for yourself by using a leg pillow to reposition your lower spine to reduce pain. Your hips will align, and your lower back will be in a better position when you place a pillow between your legs.

Use A Fan

You need an air circulator in your bedroom to cool things down and help you feel free and relaxed. Plug in a fan for this purpose. This tip is especially useful during the summer months when the temperature of your room will be higher.

Avoid Nicotine Late in The Night

Just like caffeine, nicotine is a stimulant. In other words, it works to keep you active. Taking it might help during the day, but it will be counterproductive in the night. It will affect your sleep by keeping you awake for more than you want.

Wear Socks

If you have cold feet, you will find it challenging to sleep because your body will be struggling to regulate the remaining parts of your body. So, you might need to wear socks to ensure that you keep your feet warm to get a restorative night rest.

Invest In A White Noise Machine

If you are living in an environment with consistent traffic noise, you might find it challenging to sleep. Indeed, you might end up getting used to it in the long run. However, in the meantime, you can buy a white noise machine. Research has proven that patients in an ICU slept better when exposed to white noise. Parents also usually use this machine to put a cranky baby to sleep. (8)

Get Starscape

If you have experienced the delight of sleeping out under the stars in a sleeping bag before, you can replicate it in your bedroom with one of the projection machines that they now sell. Different brands have unique features to satisfy customers. Choose the one you feel will be the best for you and watch the quality of your sleep improve dramatically.

Avoid Taking Sleeping Pills

Sleeping pills are short-term solutions to sleeping problems. They might help you to sleep better initially, but it is a problem when your body depends on them to sleep.

So, it is in your best interest to make lifestyle changes that can improve your sleep, rather than depend on drugs. You have been exposed to many ways you can improve the quality of your sleep in this book, apart from medication. Leverage them rather than depend on drugs.

Besides, sleeping pills have side effects, just like other medications. So, you will be doing yourself a great favour by avoiding them.

Enjoy The Sun More

Exposure to sunshine, especially in the morning, has many benefits. For example, it is a good source of vitamin D. Besides, it can help you to sleep better by resetting your body's sleep/wake cycle.

Read Yourself Into Your Dreamland

It is a wrong notion to assume that bedtime stories are only for children. Adults can also take advantage of this relaxing practice. Note that the kind of book you read determines the level of relaxation you will get from this activity.

Therefore, it is crucial that you pick a book that is simple to read with a good flow. You can ask your loved ones to recommend good ones, if you are not sure about picking a book that will be worth your time.

Research has proven that reading a six-minute bedtime story can improve the quality of your sleep. If you don't like reading, listening to an audiobook can also have the same effect. (10)

Be Grateful

Scientists have discovered that gratitude and a sense of well-being are often needed to gain restorative rest. Studies have also proven that if you practice daily gratitude, then you will experience positive physical effects.

The benefits include lower blood pressure, reduced anxiety, less depression, and better sleep. According to Robert A. Emmons, a professor of psychology at UC Davis, keeping a journal of gratitude is one of the best ways to have positive feelings, which bodes well for your desire to get restorative sleep and rest. (9)

Chapter Seven

Leveraging Yoga For Restorative Sleeps

From East to West, yoga has travelled around the world to different cultures to establish itself as a popular practice. Many people around the world are realizing the benefits of practicing yoga, and they are committing to it. It offers calmness and relaxation that makes people feel in charge of their lives again.

Practicing yoga regularly also improves sleep, among other benefits. This chapter will explore the benefits of yoga practice and how you can leverage it to have a restorative sleep.

The Link Between Yoga And Restorative Sleep

From anecdotal data and research, practicing yoga has the following benefits:

Enables You To Take A Breather

You will crash if you keep running at the pace of the modern world. You need periods when you take things slowly to come up with better strategies for enhanced performance. Yoga offers the platform to do so.

Relaxation Of The Body

Yoga brings the body into a state of tranquillity, which soothes it and makes it relaxed.

Relaxation Of The Mind

One of the best ways you can restore inner peace is by practicing yoga. This practice ensures that you focus on the moment, and that makes you let go of anxiety and depression.

Generation Of Positive Emotions

You need to see life beyond your current problems to be optimistic about the future. Yoga helps you to transcend your present issues, thereby restoring inner tranquillity.

Increased Self-Awareness

Life often threatens to make you lose sight of your abilities and strengths. However, yoga can help you take a close look at yourself and appreciate yourself again. Note that you need to value yourself to have self-confidence and self-esteem, which leads to high self-efficacy.

YOGA TIPS

Now that you understand the benefits of practicing yoga, you are set for tips that can help you practice effectively. Here they are:

Try A Variety Of Poses

Don't quit because you tried a pose and it seems you didn't achieve a reasonable result. Try different poses and choose the ones that give you the calmness and relaxation you crave. Besides, you should try a pose for an extended period before evaluating its effectiveness.

Use Accessories

Do all you can to get the best out of your yoga practice. Leverage pads, straps, blankets, pillows, bolsters, or blocks to support yourself for an extended period. Nothing should stop you or discourage you from achieving the sense of peace and calmness you desire.

Choose Somewhere Quiet And Free From Distractions

You should practice somewhere you can concentrate to have the best yoga experience. Physical and mental relaxation is only possible when you are in a quiet environment.

Practice For A Specified Period

You can start practicing yoga for ten to fifteen minutes. Increase it later if you want more. Nonetheless, ensure that you are consistent.

Chapter Eight

Sign In And Out In Grand Style

Sleep is an upgrade on rest. Nonetheless, you need both for sleep to be restorative. The truth is that you cannot have restorative rest without restorative sleep. They are two sides of the same coin that cannot exist independently. So, you should be working on both, rather than on one, to have the best experience.

In this last chapter, we will reiterate the benefits of restorative sleep and also some crucial sleep-related concepts you need to understand to deepen your knowledge about this topic.

Why You Need Restorative Sleeps And Rest

When you are sleeping, your body is carrying out a lot of activities, including repairing your muscles.

It also carries out some processes and metabolisms, such as digestion and the breakdown of substances ingested. These activities are responsible for the hangover effect you have in the morning after heavy drinking the previous night. Your body will try to ensure that the substance does not affect your organs, by converting it to a beneficial form.

So, you will reduce the pressure on your bodily system by drinking moderately. Your body also repairs your cells and mental functions when you are sleeping. Therefore, having a restorative sleep enhances your learning abilities and memory. It also enhances your ability to manage stress and your emotions successfully.

Note that you will be able to make better decisions when you have control over your stress levels and your emotions. Meanwhile, when you make quality decisions, you will get better results, which bodes well for your mental and physical health.

However, you cannot enjoy these benefits if you don't enter deep and REM sleep. This stage of sleep is when the body and mind truly come together. Experts refer to them as the 'restorative sleep' phase. Therefore, it is crucial that we explore them.

REM SLEEP

REM sleep is interesting in various ways. It stands for Rapid Eye Movement sleep. During this stage, your body is not active, but your mind is carrying out a lot of activities. These actions are the reason you have dreams, and sometimes, nightmares.

For some people, their bodies act in similar ways during REM as it does when they are awake. The body is shut down. However, it will still exhibit restricted movements. Experts believe that this phase of sleep is needed for emotional processing of events and memory formatting. Studies have shown that REM sleep improves our ability to develop new skills and learn. (10)

Deep Sleep

Your blood pressure and breathing rate are crucial factors that show that you have entered into a deep sleep. In a deep sleep phase, your heart rate and blood pressure will start slowing down. Brain waves in this stage are also slow and enlarged.

You need to get to this phase to enjoy restorative physical and emotional rest. When you are in a deep sleep, hormones in your body, that promote growth and healing, will be released. Besides, your immune system also gets stronger, and your body will go through a complete renewal process. (9)

When you don't sleep at night, your body will struggle to attain deep sleep the following night. The good news is that you can still catch up if you improve the quality of your sleep subsequently.

In ideal conditions, you will be in the deep sleep phase for the first third of the night, while the final part will be made up of REM sleep. Sleep experts recommend that you sleep seven to nine hours a night. However, you will not need to sleep that much to feel rejuvenated and rested as you grow older.

How To Sign In And Out In Style

As we start to conclude this book, let's explore some crucial tips that can help you sleep peacefully and wake up rejuvenated. Here they are:

Have A Stable Sleep Schedule

As earlier mentioned, you will not need to sleep up to seven to nine hours to feel refreshed as you grow older. Nonetheless, you have to maintain a consistent sleep schedule.

You will give your body the needed stability to carry out its activities when you have a regular time you sleep and wake up. When you sleep at a particular time every day, you will realize that you will wake up around the same period, even without an alarm.

Watch Out For Sleep Stealers

The quality of your sleep is not only affected by the things you do before you sleep but your general activities during the waking day. For example, drinking caffeine and alcohol are potential sleep stealers.

Regular exercise can improve the quality of your sleep. However, it can steal your sleep when it is excessive. It can lead to body pain, which prevents you from enjoying a restorative sleep. So, ensure that you are not involved in activities that can take their toll on your night's rest during the day.

LEARN THE ART OF RELAXATION

All through this book, what you have been learning is the art of relaxation. Don't allow society to put pressure on you to rush such that you forget how to rest. If you don't allow your body to rest, it will force you to do it. How? When you fall sick.

You are not a machine. Even machines have to be maintained to prevent them from breaking down. So, you need to start taking your sleep and rest seriously. You already have the information you need to change your life.

It is now time to put in practice what you have learned. There is no point in reading this book if you are not ready to utilize the information in it. So, leverage the tips you have learned and apply it to your life. You are about to have a new lease on life, by having more restorative sleep, seamlessly, as you do so.

Index

1. Michigan Medicines C.S. Mott Children's Hospital Stress Management: Relaxing You, By: Healthwise Staff, Patrice Burgess, MD, FAAFP - Family Medicine & Kathleen Romito, MD – Family. Published: December

https://www.mottchildren.org/health-library/uz220

2. Michigan Medicines C.S. Mott Children's Hospital Stress Management: Stress Management: Doing Guided Imagery to Relax. By: Patrice Burgess, MD, FAAFP - Family Medicine & Kathleen Romito, MD - Family Medicine & Adam Husney, MD - Family Medicine & Christine R. Maldonado, Ph.D. - Behavioral Health. Published: December 15, 2009...

https://www.mottchildren.org/health-library/uz2209

3. Effect of continuous heat exposure on sleep stages in humans. By: Liberty JP, Di Nisi J, Fukuda H, Muzet A, Ehrhart J, Amoros C. Published: 1989.

https://www.mottchildren.org/health-library/uz2209

4. Effects of playing a computer game using a bright display on presleep physiological variables, sleep latency, slow-wave sleep, and REM sleep.

By: J Higuchi S, Motohashi Y, Liu Y, Maeda A.

Published: 2005.

https://pubmed.ncbi.nlm.nih.gov/16120101/

5. The impact of light from computer monitors on melatonin levels in college students. Neuro Endocrinol Letter

Published: 2011. https://www.researchgate.net/publication/51107485_The_impa

ct_of_light_from_computer_monitors_on_melatonin_levels_in_college_students

6. YouGov America: 40% of Americans don't generally wake up feeling well-rested

By: Jamie Ballard.

Published: March 13, 2019.

American Kennel Club (AKC): Where do Dogs Sleep at Night

By: Erika Mansourian.

Published: August 5, 2015.

https://www.akc.org/expert-advice/lifestyle/where-dogs-sleep-night/#:~:text=In%20fact%2C%20the%20majority%20of,crate%20their%20dog%20at%20bedtime.

7. Effect of white noise on sleep in patients admitted to coronary care.

By: Farokhnezhad Afshar P, Bahramnejad F, Asgari P, and Shiri M J Caring Sci.

Published 2016.

https://www.ncbi.nlm.nih.gov/pmc/articles/PMC4923834/#:~:text=A%20study%20by%20Stanchina%20et,noises%20recorded%20in%20ICU%20environment

8. Why it Pays to Read

By: Rebecca Gross.

Published: January 16, 2015.

https://www.arts.gov/art-works/2015/why-it-pays-read

9. Understanding Sleep

By: Institute's Brain Resources and Information Network (BRAIN)

Published: 2019,

https://www.ninds.nih.gov/Disorders/Patient-Caregiver-Education/understanding-Sleep

10. Sleep Disorders,

By: National Cancer Institute

Published: 2020.

https://www.cancer.gov/about-cancer/treatment/side-effects/sleep-disorders-hp-pdq

MONEY MACHINE

A *Quick & Easy Beginner's* All-Ages Guide to Stock Market Investing & Building Passive Income
WITHOUT THE RISK OF TRIAL & ERROR

Sensei Paul David

Money Machine

A Quick & Easy Beginner's All-Ages Guide to Stock Market Investing & Building Passive Income Without the Risk of Trial & Error

Sensei Paul David

CONTENTS

FOREWORD 209

INTRODUCTION 215
   Purpose & Value of This Book 215
   My story 217

CHAPTER 1: INTRODUCTION 222
   1.1 What is Money? 222
   1.2 What is Investing? 223
   1.3 Why Is This Book Important? 223

CHAPTER 2. WORK ON YOUR INVESTMENT ATTITUDE 225
   Chapter 2.1: Control Your Money Mindset 225
   Chapter 2.2: Understand & Control Your Equity Emotions
   232
   Chapter 2.3: Adopt & Maintain a Relaxed and Long-Term Discipline 234
   Chapter 2.4: Risks to Avoid 238
   Chapter 2.5: Positions to Invest in and their Nature 244

CHAPTER 3. TOOLS AND RESOURCES. 246
   Chapter 3.1: Websites to Help You Get Started Investing
   246
   Chapter 3.2: Common Sense Advice for Picking Positions
   254
   Chapter 3.3: Practical Tips for Getting Started 256

CHAPTER 4: BASIC STRATEGIES 257
   Chapter 4.1 Diversify your investments 257
   Chapter 4.2: Don't Spend More than You Earn. 258
   Chapter 4.3: Devote a certain amount of money per month

to building your money machine.................................. 260
Chapter 4.4: Think about Asset allocation.................... 263
Chapter 4.5: Build Up Your Emergency Savings......... 264
Chapter 4.6: Debt... 265

CHAPTER 5: VOICES OF WISDOM 266
Ray Dalio 266
Paul Tutor Jones... 267
Peter Lynch 269
Robert Kiyosaki 270
Sir John Templeton 270
Warren Buffet 271
Mark Cuban 272
Jack Bogel.. 272
Benjamin Graham 273

CHAPTER 6: STAND ON THE SHOULDERS OF GIANTS.... 275
Rich Dad, Poor Dad By Robert Kiyosaki 275
Rich Dad's Cashflow Quadrant By Robert Kiyosaki .. 277
Secrets of the Millionaire Mindset By T. Harv Eker ... 278
Think & Grow Rich By Napoleon Hill 280
You Are a Badass at Making Money By Jen Sincero.. 281
The Millionaire Fastlane By MJ DeMarco 282
The Automatic Millionaire By David Bach.................. 284
The Wealthy Barber By David Chilton 285
The Richest Man in Babylon By George Clason......... 286

CHAPTER 7: INVEST LIKE THE PROS 289
7.1 Warren Buffett (Berkshire Hathaway)................... 289
7.2 Ray Dalio (Bridgewater).. 290

CHAPTER 8: CONCLUSIONS 292
REFERENCES... 294

Foreword

Sensei Paul David

Sensei Paul David gained much of his financial knowledge working as a Financial Services Project Manager for State Street Global Bank for seven years. He has also gained personal experience and financial expertise through his experience with investing for more than a decade. In this book, Sensei Paul takes the wealth of financial and investment knowledge he has gained in his professional and personal life, through his own experience and learning from the greats, to offer the reader a simplified version of the seemingly complex investment concepts such as compounding and market fluctuations. He teaches the reader how to model stock picks after famous experts, without having to be an expert yourself. Sensei David's method is to teach the reader how to transform the uncertainty they have about risk into a curiosity to learn and form the habits necessary for continuous financial self-education.

I Learned the Hard Way So You Don't Have To!

In my early 20's I worked very hard to aggressively save my money for years. I spent a while investing in mutual funds, at this point in my life, until I realized how fees were eating away at my wealth and disavowed mutual funds forever. In my efforts to increase my wealth through investing, I took the advice my father gave me to invest all of my savings into a house, fix that house up, and then rent it to build equity. At that point I didn't know anything about investing in property and believed that my father would take the reins, advising me throughout the process. I followed his advice without question. I spent over a year searching for a home to purchase, looking at over 80 homes in various cities, learning as much as I could in the process.

At 27 I finally found the home that seemed perfect. It was a fixer-upper bungalow in a strange part of a far-away suburb. From the outside, the house was an all-brick gem. It was settled in a smaller subdivision near a local General Motors plant. In my naïveté, I thought this was the perfect location, in a quaint area, near a seemingly ample supply of qualified and interested renters. I dedicated all of my free time I could find outside of my fulltime job (3 cities away) to renovating the home. I renovated the main floor moderately and focused most of my energy fixing up the basement. I created a beautiful, comfortable 2-family dwelling with zero experience. With only my wit, my mother, my friends, and unimaginable stress – covered by smiles – I managed this feat with almost no investment in renovations.

After only one year, I realized my renters had declared war on each other. A landlord's worst nightmare had come true. My tenants were using my home as a battleground to exact revenge on another in their feud. There was a kitchen fire, income cheques were stolen from, and by both families (this was before direct deposit was the norm), garbage was strewn all over the property and both families refused to pay rent. Having no money, I had to learn quickly how to act as my own lawyer. I took both families to small claims court to force them to pay what they owed me. I was also forced to call the marshal to have both families removed from the property so I could begin repairs. I had won both battles, but I was far from a celebratory mood. To top off this horrific experience, one day while I was cleaning the now empty house, I found that the tenants had made threats against me and I was forced to call 911. This whole experience took so much out of me that my family doctor recommended I go on leave from work to get my life in order and I took her advice.

It took another full year to sell the house, after both families were removed, and the property was repaired. At the end of the day, I had lost 3 years of my life, all of my investment, and my confidence. It took me a long time to recover emotionally and financially from this experience, but I decided not to be defeated. I picked myself up and learned another way to invest. I learned how to make passive income without the anxiety of an "all or nothing" approach like what my father had advised. I realized that what my father had taught me was not the way for me. At this point in my life, I now know more than my father (may he rest in peace) could have ever taught me about wealth management. An old adage says "you teach the business you know" and my experience has proven this true.

Now, after personal experience, gained from bad and good investments, self-teaching, and my career, I am here to offer to teach any who are genuinely curious (and understandably cautious – as I was when I was a financial novice) the business I know (and am continually learning). This book is written to speak to beginners, understanding that this is a new territory for you to explore. Luckily, the pattern of success in this area leaves clues. It is these clues that I have tested and will share with you in this book. My hope is that you will take this knowledge and put it into action in your life. The most successful investors on the planet all believe that there's no time to waste when it comes to getting started on investing, so let's begin!

What This Book Gives the Reader

This book promises to provide the reader with four things:

1. A single resource for a streamlined synopsis from many of the most

successful investment books and using the most successful investors' strategies.
2. A path to action, which includes the mindset and broker tools you need to consider, and advice on how to hold onto more money by avoiding long-term fees.
3. A simple resource guide written in plain English to support and coach you every step of the way, whenever you need advice or insight.
4. A FREE specialized bonus guided meditation to recap the finer points of this book in a faster and easier way than ever before.

Introduction

"An investment in knowledge pays the best interest."
Benjamin Franklin

PURPOSE & VALUE OF THIS BOOK

This book is designed to work as a reference and guide to provide you with insights from the best investors on earth, so that you can create and implement an investment strategy that will "make money work for you" (in the words of Robert Kiyosaki). This book is intended for those who have never invested, as well as those who are already dabbling in the market.

This book will help you cultivate a wealth-focused, financially smart mindset and will teach you tips, tricks, and skills that you can use to expertly manage your money and create a "money machine" that works 24/7,

365 days a year, to build wealth for you and your legacy.

The "money machine" metaphor refers to a wealth-producing system that works passively and is built from a broad portfolio of held investments that compound and produce a stream of income.

This book leverages and condenses the insights and lessons from giants in wealth production and financial guidance. This labour-unintensive guide combines and condenses this sage advice into one pithy guide, saving you time, money, and mental energy, while providing you access to the lessons of top earners and teachers in investment and money-making.

My Story

To quote a well-known US song, "I wish I knew what I know now when I was younger." Ten years ago, when I began investing, knowing the information I will provide to you in this book, would have saved me a lot of energy and disappointment. I may not have fallen into the same financial pitfalls, specifically around my investment property, had I known then what I know now.

That is the goal of this book: to share the wisdom I have gained through my own experience investing, as well as the knowledge I gained working as a project manager for the global US Institutional Bank at State Street, combined with the wisdom of other financial giants, to provide a condensed, comprehensible, and effective guide to investment and money-making. This book will give you insider access to the information, habits, and strategies that I learned and tested in my work in the world of investments.

I will always be a student in this area—though, as many of the greatest financial thinkers would seem to agree, financial education is always an ongoing process. However, this does not mean that I am not equipped to also be a teacher. I am passionate about distilling what I've learned in my research and practice, to inspire people of all ages across the world to cultivate an appetite for financial knowledge and to use this knowledge to take the leap into the realization of their wealth-production potential. I want others to become as excited as I am to be a lifelong learner in personal money management and to continue to pay this information forward.

The key benefit of this book lies in the pool of knowledge from which its lessons are drawn. This book provides a condensed and simplified collection of knowledge, advice, and techniques from financial experts across a range of disciplines. This book brings together, and puts on a silver platter for you, the wisdom of the most successful investment experts, including:

- Jack Bogel
- Benjamin Graham
- Peter Lynch
- Robert Kiyosaki
- Warren Buffett

- Ray Dalio
- Carl Icahn

This book will serve people of all ages and circumstances who want to access and implement the most secure, simple, economical, effective, enjoyable strategies and practices for "making your money work for you." This guide will provide you with the groundwork you need to take hold of your financial future and build your net worth. This guide will help you recognize and seize control over your fears and follies, giving you a guide to mimic the habits of financial experts.

DISCLAIMER:

I am not a financial advisor. While I have gained financial knowledge and know-how through my own experience and self-teaching, I am not a professional expert. The information and tips included in this guide are meant as advice based upon my own experience and are not a guarantee of financial success.

This book contains affiliate links. If you use these links to buy something, we may earn a commission. Thanks

Thank You from The Author: Sensei Paul David

Before we dive in, I'd like to thank you for picking up this book. Your time is valuable, and I know there are many other similar books out there, but you chose to invest in mine, and that means everything to me.

Now that you're here, and if you stick with me, I promise to make our time together valuable and worthwhile.

In the pages ahead, you will find some areas of information and practices more helpful than others - and that's great because as you apply what works best for you. You will benefit from an exciting transformation of character and knowledge. Enjoy!

Chapter 1: Introduction

"Don't gamble. Take all your savings and buy some good stock and hold it until it goes up, then sell it. If it doesn't go up, don't buy it."
Will Rogers

1.1 WHAT IS MONEY?

Money is the representation of the exchange in value. For consumers, value means the quality of a product or service—for example, the amount of labour and/or time required to make it, the quality of materials used, or the rarity or desirability of the product or service. This is why higher quality objects, that are more highly sought after, cost more money. For business owners, value is the ability to help solve or prevent problems as quickly, easily, and economically as possible. For example, it is the ability to repair failing equipment, technology, or systems. It is also the ability to invest in new properties, or equipment or employees of a business, to keep pace with demand.

1.2 What is Investing?

Investing is a venture—often, an adventure—in helping many types of companies add value to many customers.

When you invest in various companies, you get to ride 'piggyback' on these companies' long term successes, to receive little gifts of money, that you give to more companies, to receive more and more gifts of money, over and over again. You become part of a community of financially educated people and can share your future experiences and learnings with others, to help them learn about investing as well.

1.3 Why Is This Book Important?

In investing, you'll want to first understand the following:

- Learn to manage your money yourself to cut down on the fees and taxes you pay to advisors.

- Achieve financial literacy and learn to feel comfortable dealing with your finances and making financial decisions.
- Gain insight into different types of income—earned, portfolio, and passive—and how they are taxed.
- Learn why passive income is important.

This book will help you get started with these topics, and more, to help you best manage your portfolio and overall finances.

Chapter 2. Work on Your Investment Attitude

Humans are not rational creatures. Our decisions are often driven by emotions and it takes effort to learn how to make good decisions. This chapter discusses ways to invest more rationally and improve your "investment attitude."

CHAPTER 2.1: CONTROL YOUR MONEY MINDSET

"The market serves, it does not instruct!" (Warren Buffett)

WHY INVEST?

There are four key reasons to begin investing. First, market growth is steady over time. This may seem counterintuitive given that almost everyone alive today has seen at least one, maybe as many as three recessions and even depression. However, in the long run, increases in overall market value are as dependable as taxation. While the market may ebb and flow, over the course of years and more so over decades, if you invest intelligently, you will see a return.

Second, throughout each year you give money away without a return, you should be getting some back for yourself. With every paycheck, you hand a portion of your money away in taxes, likely with a grumble, but nonetheless, you do it without a fight. Why not hand a portion of your money to your future self by investing? In this way regularly putting money into investments is a sort of self-taxation, but (if done correctly) one in which you will see that money come back—and then some.

Third, you work for your money and, in turn, the owners or CEOs of that business profit in the process. Why not run your own investment business and return a profit for yourself? Investing is basically owning a business in which your investments are your employees, working by themselves, with your financial foundation, to produce profit for you. Get your money to work for you instead of working for your money—this is the wealth mentality.

Fourth and finally, you should invest because of the potential to earn significant profits from dividends. Although there are stocks that do not offer dividends, most stocks return dividends on a quarterly basis (every three months) and some offer an annual or monthly dividend.

The only way to make your money work for you is to add massive value by supporting and owning a piece of other businesses, thus piggybacking on their gains and cutting your losses while you make money—increasing a variety of multiple dividend returns for the rest of your life, 24 hours a day, 365 days a year.

What Are Dividends?

Dividends are a distribution of a company's earnings to shareholders. Dividends are measured in terms of their yield—that is, how much money you get. They are typically distributed as a small percentage of the overall stock's value (typically, about 2-3%, but some dividend stocks can offer closer to a 6% yield), once or several times a year. Essentially, dividends are icing on the cake: extra (free) money on top of your increase in a portfolio's worth when stock values eventually rise.

How Should You Invest: Mindset?

To quote Warren Buffet's statement that is as valuable as it is short: "Think independently." There is no one best way to invest—though don't confuse this with saying that there is no wrong, because there are plenty. However, you have to focus on finding the best way to invest intelligently, and relatively securely, in a way that works for your income level, goals, principles, and lifestyle.

That being said, *every* investment strategy should be comprehensive, regardless of what you invest in and how much you invest. You need to be in the mindset of carefully watching where your money is going and what you are getting in returns. As the saying goes, "Take care of the pennies and the dollars will take care of themselves."

To do this, you must view your role as a part-owner of what you invest in. This includes the realization that you cannot control consumer behaviour (the market).

While you can guarantee that over time the market will grow in value, no one can predict what will happen with the market, or when, at any particular point in time. Any expert who claims to be able to predict exact market behaviour at a specific time is either lying or delusional. The only guarantee is that without investing you will not receive a return.

How Should You Invest: Money?

In order for your money to work as a profitable business, you must set aside a portion of your income that is earmarked for investment, and this purpose must be non-negotiable, no matter what. You must treat your investment funding with the same sense of necessity that you treat paying rent or taxes or buying groceries.

This is the most important rule of building your money machine. Without putting your money into investments, you can never tap the power of compounding interest returns -- what Albert Einstein has called "the eighth wonder of the world," as he says, "He who understands it, earns it; he who doesn't, pays it.".

Becoming an expert in personal finance will not only give you the power of knowledge, but it will save you a significant amount of money, money that you can turn into investments, thus redoubling the financial value of handling your own finances and investments. Handling your own finances and investments not only renders you in complete control of your financial destiny, but it will save you from the fees—stated and hidden—associated with paying a financial advisor, an expense that can add up significantly over the years.

How Should You Invest: Portfolio?

Sometimes the best way to explain something is through analogy. Your portfolio is like a litter of puppies. Stick with me here, imagine you have a litter of puppies. Each puppy is different from the others, some grow faster than others, some require more food than others, but they all grow. Further, if you play your cards right and make intelligent choices with your behaviour, you can raise them to aid you however you need.

Your stock portfolio is like this litter of puppies, in that each instrument in your portfolio is unique, requiring different amounts of "sustenance" (funding) and growing at different rates. However, as you keep "feeding" these instruments with funding, as time passes, your investments will naturally grow bigger and stronger. These investments will come to serve and protect you, your home, and your legacy from harm, like a pack of guard dogs.

> *"I work to learn how to make money with money. I don't work for money, money works for me."*
> Robert Kiyosaki

Chapter 2.2: Understand & Control Your Equity Emotions

Almost everyone learns to feel an emotional attachment to their money. This makes perfect sense. Money is, after all, a representation of value. For the worker, their income is the representation of the arduous work that they put in to earn that money. In an immediate sense, money represents hours of labour and stress. However, this is only the sole representation of money for those who don't understand the power of investing. For those who do, money also represents the potential for exponentiated wealth.

Part of the emotional fear of parting with money for investment, comes from misinformation or misunderstanding (or downright lack of information) from school, families, friends -- many if not most people do not have a proper financial education. Your avoidance of investing your money needs to stop here. You need to let go of the emotional attachment and act logically and intelligently to use the market, which means using some of your income in the market, to make your money make money.

The key to overcoming this fear, and the key to significant financial growth in the market, is to remember that you are playing the long (waiting) game. Building your financial wealth will not happen overnight in the sense that you will likely not wake up tomorrow and be a millionaire, unless you get a sizable inheritance. However, it can happen while you sleep, if you invest intelligently and automate your investments.

The most important thing to remember is to be patient and know that while short-term downfalls (crashes) may occur, overall, the market is stable and day-to-day or month-to-month profit and loss do not determine income in the long run. This is not to say that you will not see growth in the short term, but it is to say that you need to be ready to persist despite what seem like immediate setbacks or stagnations.

The goal is to focus on building a money machine that will make you money "while you sleep" (automatically) and that will return significant long-term income (not cash in your pocket right away). Reassure yourself you are taking control and leveraging your money while you sleep. Approximately 30% of your life is spent sleeping, so if you live to be 90 and never invested you would have wasted 30 years of time you could have been making returns. Keep Telling yourself this is a slow process especially at first—and that's okay.

CHAPTER 2.3: ADOPT & MAINTAIN A RELAXED AND LONG-TERM DISCIPLINE

GO ULTRA-LONG

The key to investing is to be in it for the long haul. One thing that can help you with your mindset is understanding compounding for both fees and dividend yield returns.

It can be useful to automate your contributions any way you can—to "set it and forget it" to help keep your mind off the ups and downs of the market. Most financial websites allow you to make recurring contributions on a weekly, monthly, or even annual basis. You will need to connect your financial brokerage account with your bank account to be able to do this, so make sure you have enough money each time the automatic contribution is taken out.

Understand Compound Interest and the Effects of Time on Investing in General

You may want to assess your contributions in terms of your age. Young people in their 20s and 30s often are working entry-level jobs and can't afford to make a lot of contributions, but because of compounding, any amount you invest could be greatly magnified, as it will be accruing interest over a longer period. People in their 40s and above may have more money, due to their longer time in the job market and more experienced, higher-paying jobs, but will have less time for the interest to accrue, so it may be possible to contribute more. So you will want to take age into account in coming up with an investment strategy.

Understand compounding for both fees and dividend yield returns.

When it comes to fees, they add up over the years and can impede the growth of your Money Machine. The below graph is an illustrative example, depicting the loss in return that can occur with a compounding fee rate of just 2%.

Costs can eat away at your investments

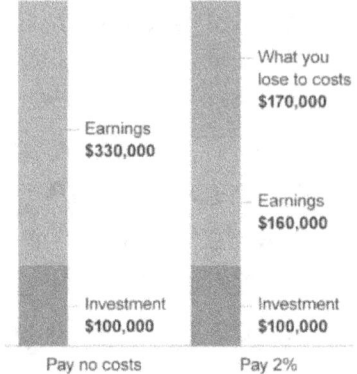

This hypothetical illustration doesn't represent any particular investment nor does it account for inflation. "What you lose to costs" represents both the amount paid in expenses as well as the "opportunity costs"—the amount you lose because the costs you paid are no longer invested. There may be other material differences between investment products that must be considered prior to investing. Numbers are rounded.

(Source: Vanguard "The Impact of Investment Costs")

On the other hand, compounding is your friend when it comes to dividend investing. Take the following example. Assume, for a given period of time, that the stock price remains relatively stable. You buy the stock, knowing that it has a relatively stable price and gives a good dividend (Tip: utilities stocks can be great for this). Then, you receive a dividend. The value of your investment is now 103% of its initial value. When another dividend rolls around, you get another 3% of your 103% back—which is an additional 3.09%. So, after two rounds of a 3% dividend, your investment is now 106.09% of its original value.

Higher dividend rates produce exponentially higher growth in returns. If your dividend yield is 5% then the first dividend increases that to 105%, with the second 5% dividend increasing your investment value to 110.25%. This increase is known as the dividend growth rate, and the higher the dividend growth rate, the better.

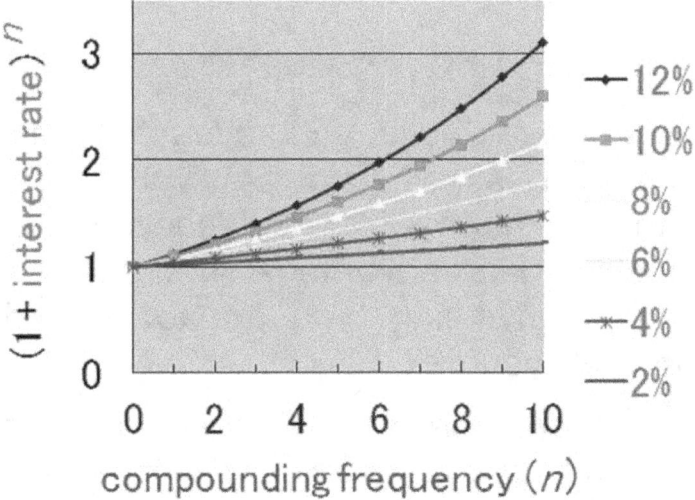

As the above graph illustrates, a higher compound interest rate helps you build your Money Machine more rapidly. (Source: Wikipedia)

You can think of compound interest as a small snowball that eventually collects enough snow to become a larger snowball. Compound interest applied to long term investing builds momentum for your portfolio and helps ensure excellent returns. Time is your friend in the compound investing game. With this type of investing, you can invest, and continuously learn and optimize. A few years later, you will find that your money machine has improved mainly by itself.

MAKE INVESTING A REQUIRED EXPENSE.

As discussed above, you have to pay taxes every year, so why not pay yourself and make it a non-negotiable aspect of your finances? The advantage is that, unlike taxes, in investing, you get to keep the money for yourself.

The challenge here is to figure out a system that works for you. The 50/30/20 rule can be helpful here—use 50% of your after-tax pay on things you need, 30% on things you want, and 20% on savings.

CHAPTER 2.4: RISKS TO AVOID

DON'T ACT ON YOUR INSTINCTS.

Don't give up, sell, or buy, without thinking ahead. This is also known as consequential thinking. What would be the benefit of your desired actions? What would be the disadvantages? Think it through before you make a decision.

Figure out how much you'll make when you sell (make sure to take into account any taxes or fees), including long-term scenarios in which you could make more by staying in the market. Work out these scenarios in your head before you buy, sell, or give up.

It's important to remember that, sometimes, the market reacts to "hype" or the latest news. These downturns are typically temporary and driven by emotional thinking which leads to sell-offs. In the long term, the market recovers from such minute corrections. Learn to take measured, strategic actions rather than emotional, drastic actions in the investment world.

DON'T IGNORE HIDDEN FEES.

Ask questions. Don't pay more than you need to. <u>Fees</u> slowly compound and slow the growth of your wealth. Here are a few examples:

A 1% fee over 1 year leaves you with 99%. Over 10 years, you will be left with just over 90% of your original investment.

1% fees over 10 years equal over 10% in lost growth.

2% fees over 10 years equal over 18% in lost growth.

3% fees over 10 years equal over 26% in lost growth.

Here, I'm just walking you through the math in a hypothetical scenario. Here's a more concrete real-world example:

Using the SEC graph below, we can see how seemingly minor increases in fee rates can drastically erode your take-home from investments over time.

With an initial investment of $100,000 and a .5% annual fee, you will see $10,000 less in returns over 20 years compared to a .25% annual fee. When the fee doubles to 1%, this loss triples to $30,000 after 20 years.

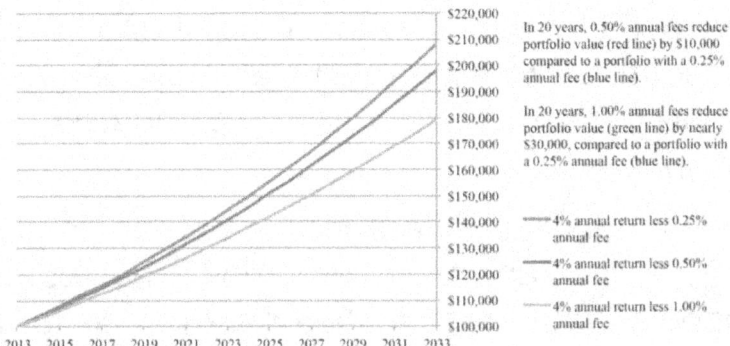

(Source: SEC "<u>Investor Bulletin: How Fees and Expenses Affect Your Investment Portfolio</u>")

DON'T IGNORE TAX RULES.

Educate yourself regarding your government's tax laws and how they pertain to affecting your investments when you withdraw funds, when you leave funds, and when you reinvest. Write down your questions and call your revenue agency and speak to an expert. Write down their answers!

INVEST IN YOURSELF.

Maximize your investment in yourself by minimizing your losses to fees. This is the key to lowering and eliminating fees.

Mutual funds can bring good returns but have high fees. On the other hand, cash accounts, like a bank savings account, can underperform over time, compared to stocks.

Fees make a difference. As a kid in the 1980s in Canada, I remember that some people would rent a stationary phone for a low monthly fee, and some people would buy a stationary phone for a noticeable, but not outrageously high, one-time fee. The people who bought the phone made an investment and didn't continue to pay for it. But the people who rented the phone were paying a pernicious fee for years, never noticing the hundreds and thousands of dollars given away over many years—dollars that could have been slowly compounded to help, instead of unknowingly eating away at their savings over the years.

Invest in yourself and you'll see the metaphorical and literal dividends materialize.

Understand the Nature of the Stock Market.

The stock market can be viewed as analogous to the weather and seasons. Weather is short-term and unpredictable, while seasons are longer-term and approximately predictable. The same goes for the stock market. Changes happen due to news and hype, which are in the short-term. The longer-term trends are more predictable and operate in an approximate 10-year cycle.

A "bull market" is a market that is expected to rise, increasing the value of investments. On the other hand, a "bear" market is a market that decreases the value of investments 20% or more from recent highs, causing pessimism for others about the future. Historically, there's roughly an approximate 10-year cycle of a bull market, followed by an approximate 2 years of a bear market.

In a bear market, stocks are down, and dividend yields increase (which pay you more money). Bear markets are actually a great time to buy because most or all the positions (stocks) go on sale—and a lucky time to get started in investing. However, time in the market, beats timing the market, ultimately—meaning that any time is a great time to start investing.

In a bull market, when stocks show a pattern of improvement, dividend yields decrease (which pay you less money). Bear markets are a great time for investors—assuming the investments are reliable (blue chip) stocks that show many years of never having missed a dividend distribution (or payout). This can be easily checked online nowadays.

Basis points are a common measurement unit for interest rates. One basis point is the equivalent of 1/100th of 1%, as Investopedia defines it. A 1% change, therefore, is 100 basis points.

CHAPTER 2.5: POSITIONS TO INVEST IN AND THEIR NATURE

When you buy an investment, you can say you have taken a position in it, whether it is a company, property, fund, or another type of investment. When considering positions to invest in, you should consider all the different possibilities for the best outcomes. Here are a few different positions:

- **Vanguard Index funds** were founded by finance guru Jack Bogle in the 1970s. They are more expensive and do not pay out as much but tend to be more reliable. Index funds are designed to mirror a market index, so you end up becoming an owner in the market.
- **Real Estate Investment Trusts or REITs** include property or mortgage. This can include apartments, office buildings, and retail spaces.
- **Exchange-Traded Funds or ETFs** are pre-picked baskets of funds, but they won't make you rich.
- **Individual stocks** may make you more money, but they may or may not survive a bear market, so you need to do your research.

Chapter 3. Tools and Resources.

"A successful man is one who can lay a firm foundation with the bricks others have thrown at him."
David Brinkley

CHAPTER 3.1: WEBSITES TO HELP YOU GET STARTED INVESTING

Many large banks allow you to open investment brokerage accounts and offer to buy and to sell with little to no commissions or fees. However, there are also smaller, independent self-serve brokers that are alternatives to those offered by large banks. I prefer these smaller brokers because they are among the most user-friendly investment apps, both in terms of their interface and customer support. They are also more effective and efficient than many other investment tools, including traditional banks. The interface for these websites also appears more simple and the customer support element is faster and more effective to my mind.

- Questrade
- Wealthsimple
- Robinhood

You must do your own comparative research and make your own decision about which broker to use—and stick to that decision. However, I will offer a brief overview of each of these platforms to help you get started in your comparison.

QUESTRADE

What is Questrade?

Questrade is a mobile and desktop investment and trading platform for Canadian residents offering access to various investment products and portfolio management options at low fees.

What Can You Do on Questrade?

Questrade offers a platform for savings, investment, and trading in an array of products and markets so that you can broaden your portfolio and leverage your investments.

The Questrade platform offers you the ability to invest in:

- Stocks (long and short)
- Options (simple and multi-leg)
- Bonds (through a live broker)
- Exchange-Traded Funds (EFTs)
- Mutual Funds
- Contracts for Difference (CFDs) (requires additional platform IQ Edge)
- Forex (requires additional platform IQ Edge)

Questrade also offers savings and investment options:

- Tax-Free Savings Accounts (TFSAs)
- Registered Retirement Savings Plans (RRSPs)
- Margin Accounts for US & CDN positions
- Guaranteed Investment Certificates (GICs)
- International Equities
- Initial Public Offerings (IPOs)
- Precious Metal Purchases

Questrade offers free snapshots of basic market information, or, for an additional fee, live-streamed market updates, from top market sources, such as NYSE and NASDAQ. This simplified information snapshot shows your balances, buying power, positions, margin balances, and profit and loss. You can customize which information you are shown to make your trading decisions more efficient.

How Easy is Questrade to Use?

Questrade is designed to facilitate the investment process, offering an intuitive and simplified platform that functions the same whether you are using it on your computer or a smart device.

WEALTHSIMPLE

What is Wealthsimple?

Wealthsimple is a desktop and mobile investment and saving platform for Canadian, US, and UK residents providing algorithm-based automated portfolio management and saving services at low fees with a $0 minimum opening balance.

What Can You Do with Wealthsimple?

The Wealthsimple platform facilitates financial goal achievement by employing an algorithm, based on Modern Portfolio Theory, calculated using your responses to a questionnaire concerning:

- financial goals
- time-frame
- risk tolerance
- investment experience
- level of investment knowledge

The Wealthsimple portfolio building and management algorithm uses generic buy and hold strategies, is populated by 8-10 well-founded investment instruments, and employs tried and true market strategies including:

- diversification of asset classes
- passive buy and hold investing
- dividend reinvestment
- risk scoring
- your feedback

However, you do have some basic control over your portfolio construction. You can choose from socially conscious (e.g. eco-friendly) portfolios and Halal accounts. You can also change the proportion of your funding devoted to each instrument.

The Wealthsimple website shows your key account features and allows you to review your transactions and investment performance statistics based upon movement toward each of your financial goals. Further, Wealthsimple live representatives can be reached by phone or email (though no live chat). You can speak with a live financial advisor upon request and you can hold unlimited financial planning sessions as a member (you are allowed one session as a non-member).

Finally, Wealthsimple also provides numerous easy-to-use financial and investment education tools, including a thorough "Investing 101" glossary, a comprehensive investment FAQ page, covering common questions and concerns, and monthly blogs and magazine issues which include numerous financial and investing "How-To" discussions.

How Easy is Wealthsimple to Use?

Wealthsimple makes smart investing and saving a no-brainer. Using an algorithm that populates your portfolio with ETFs, mutual funds, or a combination (depending upon which region you live in) and determines the proportion of funds towards each, to maximize your potential to reach your financial goals, while minimizing your risk of loss. The portfolio is automatically compiled by Wealthsimple based upon your answers to their profile-building questionnaire and your selections in the pool of potential financial goals.

The Wealthsimple algorithm takes the guesswork out of investing by automatically rebalancing your portfolio based upon your progress toward your goals and following deposits, withdrawals, and changes in asset values or risk score. Wealthsimple also automatically determines the nature of your portfolio as conservative, balances, or growth-focused based upon your profile and goals.

Transfers are as easy as a few clicks of your mouse. You can transfer taxable or retirement accounts to start your Wealthsimple account, or you can deposit new funds. The website is mobile-ready and easy to read and navigate.

ROBINHOOD

What is Robinhood?

Robinhood is a mobile investment and trading platform, available as a mobile device application or traditional website. It is designed for the most novice of investors. Robinhood is noted for its simplicity, low deposit requirements (no minimum), and low stock purchase requirements (you can purchase partial shares).

What Can You Do with Robinhood?

Robinhood's key selling points are that it allows you to invest in stocks—including partial stocks – and trade in cryptocurrency with no minimum investment requirements and no trading cost. The key to the Robinhood app is its simplicity and lack of minimum funding requirements (i.e. no minimum deposit). However, because the focus of Robinhood is on simplicity, there are few if any ways to customize your profile.

How Easy is Robinhood to Use?

Robinhood is noted as one of the most user-friendly and therefore simple investment applications to use. It should be noted that some of this hyper-simplicity means that this tool does not provide the same depth of information or customization that other investment apps or websites offer. However, for the novice investor, especially the novice investor who is seeking to start small (i.e. purchasing partial shares), the Robinhood app and website is one of the simplest ways to get your feet wet in investing.

ADVANTAGES AND DISADVANTAGES OF ONLINE BROKERAGE FIRMS

In Canada, we have Wealthsimple and Questrade. Wealth simple is highly automated, but there's less opportunity for learning because of the automation. Questrade is more manual and has great customer service for learning as you go—understanding taxes, fees, products and accounts. In the United States, apps like Robinhood are also available. These apps make it easy to invest from the convenience of your smartphone.

I prefer a manual self-learning approach and I use Questrade for that reason.

CHAPTER 3.2: COMMON SENSE ADVICE FOR PICKING POSITIONS

Picking positions takes some effort and thought. It's a good idea to create a requirements checklist for identifying positions that meet your standards.

Here are some tips for creating such a checklist:

- Think long-term. Ask yourself, *what will help take care of me when I'm too old to work?*
- Do your research. Google what the company or fund does; its holdings; and its history, both in terms of performance and in terms of ventures.
- Check out the dividend payout. Examine dividend yield and payout history.
- Remember other indicators of success such as market cap and price—both over the last year and throughout a company's lifetime.

Once you've figured out your positions over the span of a few days, execute your trades. Time is of the essence of investing!

Chapter 3.3: Practical Tips for Getting Started

Here's some of my advice as a lifelong student investor:

- I believe time in the market beats timing the market. Don't try to time the market, just get started the best way you can with what you can afford at first.
- Expect fluctuations in unrealized value in the total value of your portfolio. This is normal. Hold on to what you have, and build upon it by regularly contributing to your portfolio and making consistent investments. Make sure to reinvest dividends right away—many brokers have the option to automatically reinvest dividends for you in what is called a DRIP (Dividend Reinvestment Program). I prefer not to use a DRIP but to manually allocate my funds based on stock price and yield weekly.

Chapter 4: Basic Strategies

"It takes as much energy to wish as it does to plan."
Eleanor Roosevelt

CHAPTER 4.1 DIVERSIFY YOUR INVESTMENTS

Diversifying your investments means not putting all your eggs in one basket. When you invest in a variety of different positions, you can decrease risk by having a bunch of different "baskets" so to speak. Mitigate risk by investing in a variety of different stocks. For example, you may opt for a value investment approach with a few well-researched investments in riskier positions. Consider, for example, investing in both NYSE and NASDAQ stocks so that if the NASDAQ hits a low, you still have some liquidity in the markets due to your other investments.

Diversification of investments is the best way to reduce risk and maximize gains.

"Keeping your money spread across many stocks and industries is the only reliable insurance against the risk of being wrong. But diversification doesn't just minimize your odds of being wrong. It also maximizes your chance of being right."—Ben Graham, *The Intelligent Investor*

CHAPTER 4.2: DON'T SPEND MORE THAN YOU EARN.

Analyze your monthly expenditures. When you're working on managing your finances, the most important part is to take stock of your monthly expenditures and make sure that you have the money for them. If you find yourself unable to pay the bills each month and seem to be escalating toward debt, check in with your finances.

Make a budget and see whether you can stick to it. If you cannot live within your means, you will need to cut things out of your budget or see if you can get a job that enables you to make ends meet. Making a budget and comparing it to your typical spending is a great way to stay accountable for your finances. Oftentimes, you will notice that you can cut back in some places to save money. Perhaps your shopping habit is out of control, and you are holding on to goods you can either sell or return to the store—or you just need to cut back. Maybe you've been eating too much takeout and delivery from local restaurants when you could just cook at home. Whatever your spending patterns are, figure them out—and learn from them to come up with a budget that works for you.

Chapter 4.3: Devote a Certain Amount of Money per Month to Building Your Money Machine.

Once you check in with your finances, as discussed in Chapter 3.1, you can start building your money machine. By "money machine," I mean the investment portfolio that earns you passive dividend income, which you can reinvest to make your money machine grow faster. To do this, dedicate a certain amount of money per month—that you never touch—to building your money machine. Learning the keys to financial success means learning from the wisdom of those who have managed financial success.

According to *The Automatic Millionaire*, by David Bach, those who want to be "super-rich, super-fast" should "pay themselves first" by setting aside at least 20% of their gross income. Not setting aside anything, or setting aside anything less than 5%, can set one up for being "poor" or even "dead broke."

In your journey to learn the keys to financial success, it is vital to be familiar with the greats in financial success -- to stand on the shoulders of giants, you must first know who the giants are. Jim Rohn is one of the most well-known and well-respected of these greats. He was a trail-blazing self-starter, investment and business guru, and financial mentor.

From humble beginnings as the child of Idaho farmers in mid-twentieth century, Rohn made a rapid rise to financial success and fame by his early thirties following the advice of his mentor Earl Shoaff. He has been invited to speak to audiences from high school students to Rotary Clubs, quickly expanding to paid seminars to packed audiences. Jim Rohn has also published numerous popular books and won numerous industry awards, inspiring millions with his approachable and grounded attitude to personal finance building, from an insightful human behaviour based philosophy and the mentor of world-renowned life coach Tony Robbins.

Jim Rohn suggests a fairly simple breakdown of proportions of expenditures to build a portfolio that will set you up for financial greatness which will allow you a comfortable living and still leave room for spreading the wealth so that you can build your karma while you build your wealth. He suggests devoting 70% of your income to your living expenses (bills, groceries, gas, etc.), 10% to charity, 10% to lower-risk investing, and the last 10% to higher-risk investing. This breakdown will allow you to take the necessary leaps to make meaningful gains while maintaining financial security.

However, if you can afford to devote more than 20% of your income to investing (that is if you can live off of less than 70% of your income and invest the rest), Rohn strongly suggests that you do so. Essentially, you want to devote as much of your income to investing as you reasonably can without depriving yourself of necessities and a safety net.

Especially for those who are starting out in their middle age, you will need to find ways to compound your wealth more quickly. In order to see your financial growth pay off before retirement, you will likely need to devote more than 20% of your income to invest. The more you invest, the greater your return. The more you pay into your money machine, the more you will be able to invest. The more you invest, the more your money will compound, meaning increased investments are met with exponential income growth.

CHAPTER 4.4: THINK ABOUT ASSET ALLOCATION

Dividends are usually paid out as cash payments. This means that you are free to do whatever you want with your dividend payments without having to sell your stock. Of course, you can reinvest your dividends to buy more stocks of the paying company—and this may be a wise choice if the stock is doing particularly well (more stock means more cash from dividends). However, it may be wiser yet to hold onto your dividend cash payments and use them to broaden your portfolio by buying a different stock or investment instrument. Putting your dividend cash payments in the bank to build up until the next bear market will mean that you have that much more investment power when stock prices drop (the ideal time to invest).

Chapter 4.5: Build Up Your Emergency Savings

The gold standard for savings seems to be to hold enough savings to cover six months of bills and living expenses (e.g. groceries, gas). Having this kind of savings essentially buys you six months for the economy, the market, or your current situation to stabilize (though hopefully, you would never have to use up your entire savings). Further, having sizable savings also protects you against emergencies such as home or car repairs, medical costs, or any other kind of unforeseen major expense.

Finally, having significant savings also protects you against the effects of downturns in the market (especially the shift to a bear market). As the saying goes, "time in the market beats timing the market." The market will always shift over time between a bear market and a bull market, but having savings built up means that you will be able to ride through the downturns (or life disasters or major expenses) without having to pull out of the market. If you can persevere through the bear market, you will see the reward for your perseverance when the market has an upturn and stabilizes again.

CHAPTER 4.6: DEBT

Pay your debts and pay them on time, but don't overpay them. Meaning, after paying your monthly dues for debts, pay yourself before applying any extra income toward paying off debt. This may sound counterintuitive. You may be thinking, "Won't I lose money on interest if I take longer to pay my debts?" While this may be true, one of the common pieces of advice from successful and prominent financial experts is to pay yourself first so you can focus that money on investing. Money paid toward debt is money that you are not putting into the market. Many financial experts even say that you should pay yourself before paying *anything* else. If you want to make your money work for you, you have to make paying yourself (and investing those self-payments) a non-negotiable process. Don't think twice. Don't skip any self-payment. This is the only way to see your money grow.

Chapter 5: Voices of Wisdom

"Before you speak, listen. Before you write, think. Before you spend, earn. Before you invest, investigate. you criticize, wait. Before you pray, forgive. Before you quit, try. Before you retire, save. Before you die, give."
William A. Ward

The best way to learn sage investment advice is to read the work of the experts.

RAY DALIO

"I learned that if you work hard and creatively, you can have just about anything you want, but not everything you want. Maturity is the ability to reject good alternatives in order to pursue even better ones."

"Listening to uninformed people is worse than having no answers at all."

"In trading, you have to be defensive and aggressive at the same time."

"Don't put the expedient ahead of the strategic"

"Almost nothing can stop you from succeeding if you have a) flexibility and b) self-accountability."

PAUL TUTOR JONES

"I believe the very best money is made at the market turns. Everyone says you get killed trying to pick tops and bottoms and you make all your money by playing the trend in the middle. Well for twelve years I have been missing the meat in the middle but I have made a lot of money at tops and bottoms."

"If I have positions going against me, I get right out; if they are going for me, I keep them. Risk control is the most important thing in trading. If you have a losing position that is making you uncomfortable, the solution is very simple: Get out, because you can always get back in."

"The secret to being successful from a trading perspective is to have an indefatigable and an undying and unquenchable thirst for information and knowledge."

"Don't ever average losers. Decrease your trading volume when you are trading poorly; increase your volume when you are trading well. Never trade in situations where you don't have control. For example, I don't risk significant amounts of money in front of key reports, since that is gambling, not trading."

"Intellectual capital will always trump financial capital."

Peter Lynch

"If you're prepared to invest in a company, then you ought to be able to explain why in simple language that a fifth-grader could understand, and quickly enough so the fifth grader won't get bored."

"There's no shame in losing money on a stock. Everybody does it. What is shameful is to hold on to a stock, or worse, to buy more of it when the fundamentals are deteriorating."

"If you can't find any companies that you think are attractive, put your money in the bank until you discover some."

"If you don't study any companies, you have the same success buying stocks as you do in a poker game if you bet without looking at your cards."

"In the long run, a portfolio of well-chosen stocks and/or equity mutual funds will always outperform a portfolio of bonds or a money-market account. In the long run, a portfolio of poorly chosen stocks won't outperform the money left under the mattress."

Robert Kiyosaki

"The fear of being different prevents most people from seeking new ways to solve their problems."

"If you want to be rich, you need to develop your vision. You must be standing on the edge of time gazing into the future."

"Often, the more money you make the more money you spend; that's why more money doesn't make you rich – assets make you rich."

"The moment you make passive income and portfolio income a part of your life, your life will change. Those words will become flesh."

"Find the game where you can win, and then commit your life to playing it, and play to win."

Sir John Templeton

"Bull markets are born on pessimism, grown on skepticism, mature on optimism and die on euphoria. The time of maximum pessimism is the best time to buy, and the time of maximum optimism is the best time to sell."

"The only reason to sell them a stock now is to buy other, more attractive stocks. If you can't find more attractive stocks, hold on to what you have."

"The only way to avoid mistakes is not to invest—which is the biggest mistake of all."

"Forgive yourself for your errors. Don't become discouraged, and certainly don't try to recoup your losses by taking bigger risks. Instead, turn each mistake into a learning experience. Determine exactly what went wrong and how you can avoid the same mistake in the future."

WARREN BUFFET

"It's far better to buy a wonderful company at a fair price than a fair company at a wonderful price."

"Only buy something that you'd be perfectly happy to hold if the market shut down for 10 years."

"Wide diversification is only required when investors do not understand what they are doing."

"Look at market fluctuations as your friend rather than your enemy; profit from folly rather than participate in it."

"We've used derivatives for many, many years. I don't think derivatives are evil, per se, I think they are dangerous. ...So we use lots of things daily that are dangerous, but we generally pay some attention to how they're used. We tell the cars how fast they can go."

MARK CUBAN

"One thing we can all control is effort. Put in the time to become an expert in whatever you're doing. It will give you an advantage because most people don't do this."

"It's not in the dreaming, it's in the doing."

"Creating opportunities means looking at where others are not."

"Perfectionism is the enemy of profitability."

JACK BOGEL

"In recent years, annual trading in stocks — necessarily creating, by reason of the transaction costs involved, a negative value for traders — averaged some $33 trillion.

But capital formation — that is, directing fresh investment capital to its highest and best uses, such as new businesses, new technology, medical breakthroughs, and modern plant and equipment for existing business — averaged some $250 billion. Put another way, speculation represented about 99.2% of the activities of our equity market system, with capital formation accounting for 0.8%."

"Investing is not nearly as difficult as it looks. Successful investing involves doing a few things right and avoiding serious mistakes."

"Time is your friend; impulse is your enemy."

"The index fund is a sensible, serviceable method for obtaining the market's rate of return with absolutely no effort and minimal expense. Index funds eliminate the risks of individual stocks, market sectors and manager selection, leaving only stock market risk."

BENJAMIN GRAHAM

"An investment operation is one which, upon thorough analysis, promises safety of principal and an adequate return.

Operations not meeting these requirements are speculative."

"But investing isn't about beating others at their game. It's about controlling yourself at your own game."

"People who invest make money for themselves; people who speculate make money for their brokers."

"You must thoroughly analyze a company, and the soundness of its underlying businesses, before you buy its stock; you must deliberately protect yourself against serious losses; you must aspire to "adequate," not extraordinary, performance."

"You will be much more in control if you realize how much you are not in control."

"Obvious prospects for physical growth in a business do not translate into obvious profits for investors."

Albert Einstein is reputed to have said, "**Compound interest** is the eighth wonder of the world. He who understands it earns it; he who doesn't pays it."

Chapter 6: Stand on the Shoulders of Giants

"Risk comes from not knowing what you're doing."
Warren Buffett

Money mindset books out there offer powerful advice for investors from the experts. Here are a few summaries of the best money mindset books out there.

You can find these and other books on my website here. I update this page every so often with links to my favourite books.

RICH DAD, POOR DAD BY ROBERT KIYOSAKI

In *Rich Dad, Poor Dad* Robert Kiyosaki discusses the difference in financial literacy and mentality between the rich and the poor and middle classes. Essentially, Kiyosaki holds that it is a lack of financial literacy and a mentality focused on making more money and securing that money that traps poor and middle-class individuals in the "rat race" and the cycle of debt. The poor and middle-class focus on making and keeping money through work – and securing your job as a means to this – leads them to ignore opportunities for income and financial asset growth because they are too focused on paying expenses. The mentality of "I can't afford it" shuts off creativity, the mentality of "how can I afford it" pushes you toward action. The rich focus on learning new skills and keeping their eyes and minds open to new financial opportunities. Poor and middle-class people confuse liabilities with assets – this ends up increasing their debt. Assets make you money, liabilities cost you money. For example, it is thought, among the poor and middle classes, to be an asset because of its value, but because of derivatives, taxes, upkeep, and loss in return upon selling, houses often actually lead to more debt. Rental property on the other hand is an asset: it makes you money via rent payments. Gaining financial literacy, specifically accounting, investing, and tax law, are the keys to financial success. Don't work for money, make money work for you.

RICH DAD'S CASHFLOW QUADRANT BY ROBERT KIYOSAKI

Following from the discussion of the "rich" versus the "poor" financial/work mentality discussed in *Rich Dad, Poor Dad*, in <u>Cashflow Quadrant,</u> Kiyosaki discusses the four positions in what he calls the "cashflow quadrant" – or the four means of income: 1) employee, 2) self-employed, 3) business owner, and 4) investor. It is possible to belong to more than one quadrant, in fact, this is preferred. However, each quadrant requires particular skills, so if you are going to switch quadrants or keep one foot in multiple quadrants, you will need to possess the knowledge and skills needed for each of those quadrants. Those in the first two quadrants have the most difficulty getting rich, those in the last two quadrants have the easiest time. These quadrants are defined by four factors: 1) focus on job/income security, 2) focus on the job/financial freedom, 3) amount of personal time required for income (working hours), and 4) amount of money garnered. The employee and self-employed both place the highest value on job security, trading their time for money (they work for their money), the latter experiencing less security than the former who is shielded from disasters, such as major medical issues by employee benefits. However, neither the employee nor the self-employed experiences job or income freedom and neither is likely to make one rich. The business owner and the investor focus on job and financial freedom, garnering lots of money without having to devote considerable time to their work (their money works for them).

SECRETS OF THE MILLIONAIRE MINDSET BY T. HARV EKER

T. Harv Eker's *Secrets of the Millionaire Mindset*, like the other books discussed, and as the title suggests, is a how-to guide for shifting your mindset to break old habits that keep you poor and make new ones that will help make you rich. Behaviour is learned, particularly learned from our parents. Most people learn how to get a job, what job to get, how to perceive work and holding a job, and how to save or spend our earnings from our parents and most people unconsciously replicate this learned behaviour when they are adults. The key trick to taking on the "mind of the millionaire" then is to recognize that you are in charge of how you make and spend money and to take the reins in reimagining and manifesting the mindset of the rich. In order to manifest the mindset of the rich, which allows them to make (and hold onto) their money, you must first learn to appreciate this mindset. In brief, you cannot despise a millionaire at the same time that you seek to become one. This negative mindset toward "the rich" will create a mental block and keep you from engaging with and learning from the rich. The key to gaining the "millionaire mind" is thus realizing that you are in control, taking conscious and thoughtful steps to direct your earning and spending to make more money and waste less money, and to learn to appreciate the financial wisdom that the wealthy can offer.

THINK & GROW RICH BY NAPOLEON HILL

In *Think & Grow Rich* ,Napoleon Hill puts forward the simple argument that the attainment of riches derives from a single-minded and unrelenting determination to become rich. Success and failure are both end results of and driven by mindsets of success or failure. Ultimately the attainment of wealth (getting rich) is achievable if you are able to control your own mind. The best way to achieve this control over your mind is to maintain singleness of purpose and strength of desire. Hill lays out the means of achieving and maintaining that mindset throughout this book. There are four key aspects of your goal that are necessary for its achievement. First, it must be a singular goal. Second, your goal must be definite, you must know exactly what you want to achieve (exactly how much money you want to have) and exactly how you are going to achieve (what are you going to do to get that money?). Third, you must have a burning, all-consuming, desire to achieve this goal -- this desire must predominate your thoughts and energies. Fourth, you must believe that your goal will be achieved, you must visualize its achievement and build and maintain faith that it will happen. Additionally, you must be flexible. If you're not achieving your goal through the means you have developed, make a different plan. Don't give up, persistence, driven by a perpetual burning desire to achieve your goal, must be maintained. Start today, even if you don't have a plan, begin by visualizing your goal.

YOU ARE A BADASS AT MAKING MONEY BY JEN SINCERO

In *You Are a Badass at Making Money*, Jen Sincero takes an arguably unconventional approach to what it means and what it takes to become "rich." Sincero, like Napoleon Hill, discusses quite often, the importance of putting your desire into the universe. However, what this ultimately means is that you have to give your mentality and energy toward achieving your financial goal and you have to visualize its manifestation and believe that it *will* happen. Unlike many other mainstream books about making money, that focus specifically on becoming a millionaire, and working the market or your career path to make this happen, Sincero offers a different definition. To be "rich" is to have enough money that you can live your best and most authentic life -- whatever that means to you. To achieve riches, you must thus take on a mindset focused upon this goal. In order to achieve this mindset, you must first understand why you want to get rich, what you would spend that money on, how you will make that money, and when you will achieve this goal. Your answers to the first two questions need to be more meaningful than the desire to swim in a pool of cash and buy a Lamborghini. You must then be willing to take a hard look at the habits you have that lead you to waste money and time (that you could use to make money). You must be willing to dive headfirst toward your goal.

THE MILLIONAIRE FASTLANE BY MJ DEMARCO

MJ DeMarco, in *The Millionaire Fastlane*, argues that the only dependable way to get rich is by owning your own business, specifically a business that offers a unique, valuable, and marketable product (either a commodity, for example, an appliance, or a service, such as programming). DeMarco argues that stocks are not dependable because of the threat of market crashes or the more mundane threat of a drop in stock values. Even retirement or other interest-bearing accounts are not dependable, again because of the threat of a market crash, and because of inflation which amounts to a loss of real worth ($3 million today may only be worth $1 in real value by the time you retire). Further, investing in a time-consuming and costly college degree will not only drain your financial resources but will give you a late start and will not give you the skills you need to be an adept business owner -- the skills of creativity, drive, and financial and consumer-market sense -- all of which you can learn on your own. In order to create a business that thrives without a focus on the "tried and true" those markets are already cornered and swamped with the competition. Instead, be inventive, focus on creating something new that will be in demand and meet customer needs. Finally, switch from a consumer to a business owner mindset. Examine products, advertisements and businesses through a "behind the scenes" lens, investigating their business and advertising model and the value and ingenuity of their product.

THE AUTOMATIC MILLIONAIRE BY DAVID BACH

In his book, *The Automatic Millionaire*, David Bach explains how shifting to automatic savings, investments, and bill payments, as well as cutting down on small unnecessary expenses, can make you a millionaire by the time you retire. One key point made by this book -- a theme shared with Kiyosaki -- is the value of "paying yourself first". Most people pay their bills, taxes, and other expenses first and then (hopefully) save or (better) invest what is left over. However, this is backward: you should put money into your retirement fund, rainy day fund, savings, and investments first and then deal with your bills and expenses with the remainder. Automating these savings and investments will allow this process to become second nature and change this use of money from optional to non-negotiable. Putting a percentage of your income in your savings or retirement fund before your check is cut is also a great way to save money and reduce loss of income from taxes. Equally important to "paying yourself first" and automating savings and investments, is cutting down or eliminating unnecessary small costs, such as coffee or food out or other impulse buys can increase your expendable income (and therefore your savings and investments) drastically over the course of your working life.

THE WEALTHY BARBER BY DAVID CHILTON

David Chilton's *The Wealthy Barber,* is a financial guide told through a narrative lens. The story follows the main characters as they seek out and learn the wisdom of a barber who has become wealthy through financial conservation and literacy. A recurrent theme in the financial guides discussed in this chapter, the barber advises first and most importantly to "pay yourself first". Deciding upon a meaningful, but manageable, amount of your income to set aside from each paycheck is the first step to "making your money work for you" (in the words of Kiyosaki). The barber suggests setting aside 10%—this amount is enough to build up and do something worthwhile with, but not so much that it will drastically change your lifestyle. However, building up extra cash alone will not make you a millionaire. To accomplish this goal, you have to make your money make you money, that is, you need to invest. The wealthy barber suggests putting your money into investments, like mutual funds, which, while they have a lower overall rate of return, are far more secure. The wealthy barber holds that pouring your money into stocks is essentially gambling. The wealthy barber also warns against putting your money into property or other assets that may take away from the money you are able to invest. Buying a home can provide a return if you play your cards right, but if paying your mortgage takes money out of your savings, it's a loss.

THE RICHEST MAN IN BABYLON BY GEORGE CLASON

In *The Richest Man in Babylon*, George Clason explains that the keys to accumulating wealth lie in a mindset focused on earning, saving, learning, and prudence. Clason uses pearls of wisdom from throughout history and the analogy of Babylon -- one of the richest civilizations -- to exemplify his points. Unlike many other books on cultivating a wealth-focused or "rich" mindset, Clason focuses, not on the investment side, but rather on the earning side. The key to accumulating wealth is in earning. The more you earn, the more you can save. Mastering your trade, and better, learning new trades, will expand your capacity to earn. You should also seek out advice, but make sure you are seeking out advice only from those who are financially knowledgeable and responsible. Because, as earning grows often, so does the cost of one's lifestyle, you need to maintain a simple lifestyle and save at least 10% of your earnings and use the rest for your expenses. Debt should be paid off as soon as reasonably possible -- if you are in debt 20% of your income should go to paying it off. However, while saving 10% and paying off debts, you should also not put so much money away or into debt that you deprive yourself. Adopt a frugal but reasonably comfortable lifestyle. Investing is wise if you are careful. Do not invest in ventures that do not offer a meaningful return or those that seem too good to be true.

Chapter 7: Invest like the Pros

You can follow the lead of investment professionals like Warren Buffett and Ray Dalio to succeed in the investing game and maximize your Money Machine. In this chapter, we offer insights on how to invest like these two giants of investment and finance, using public investment information from their companies.

7.1 Warren Buffett (Berkshire Hathaway)

Despite being a billionaire and one of the richest people in the world, Buffett—also known as the Oracle of Omaha—is known for living in his modest Nebraska home and avoiding spending on luxury items, opting instead for a burger and Cherry Coke as a treat.

Famous as an ultra-long value investor, Buffett eschews the new in favour of time-tested classics, such as Coca-Cola, BNSF, GEICO, and See's Candies. One exception to this rule is Buffett's investment in tech giant, Apple, maker of the popular iPhone, as well as e-commerce retailer, Amazon.

Berkshire Hathaway, Buffett's company, holds a number of popular value investments in their portfolio besides the above-mentioned companies, including American Express, Bank of America Corporation, Biogen, Costco, Davita Dialysis, General Motors Company, Johnson & Johnson, Procter & Gamble, UPS, and <u>many other</u> well-known, high-performing, and high-reputation companies.

7.2 RAY DALIO (BRIDGEWATER)

Buffett's spendthrift nature sets him apart from other investors, like Ray Dalio, who owns Bridgewater Associates, an asset management firm and the world's largest hedge fund. Dalio, a graduate of Harvard Business School, wrote a <u>132-page volume</u> on what helped him succeed in investing. Among these is the ability to accept and deal with the issues that one faces in life.

Another is listening to others and maintaining good relationships with family and friends. While money can be fleeting, relationships can be more long-lasting. Using reality as a compass, Dalio believes, can help one succeed in the investment world. Risk management is also a very large part of this strategy.

Dalio's Bridgewater invests in Biogen (like Berkshire Hathaway), as well as pharmaceutical company Bristol-Myers Squibb Company, United Rentals, Macy's, steel producer Nucor Corporation, Royal Bank of Canada, Eastman Chemical Company, and Alliance Data Systems.

Chapter 8: Conclusions

"If you don't find a way to make money while you sleep, you will work until you die."
Warren Buffett

Investing can be overwhelming. It can feel like there's a lot of information to learn, a lot of math, and you may be intimidated by the typical image of the investor that you see—a professional working on the Wall Street floor. The truth is that anyone can get started in investing. By using the right strategies and doing your research, you can make sure that you make the most of your money machine.

Investing doesn't have to be difficult. Approach investing with a curious mind. Remain eager to learn. After following the markets for a while, making various mistakes and successes, following the news, etc., you will get a feel for how it all works. There is nothing that can substitute this type of experience, so be prepared for that, and have a growth and learning mindset.

Once again, congratulations on considering or deciding to pursue a dream that few people will experience first hand. Stay excited, curious and meticulous in learning all you can—once you take action daily for six months, it may change how you define yourself.

References

Bach, David. 2016. "The Automatic Millionaire (Expanded and Updated): A Powerful One-Step Plan to Live and Finish Rich." Crown Publishing Group: New York.

Chen, James. 2020. "Dividend Growth Rate." *Investopedia*. Retrieved September 27th, 2020. https://www.investopedia.com/terms/d/dividendgrowthrate.asp

Chen, James. 2020. "Basis Points (BPS)." *Investopedia*. Retrieved September 27th, 2020. https://www.investopedia.com/terms/b/basispoint.asp

Chilton, David. 1998. "The Wealthy Barber: Everyone's Commonsense Guide to Becoming Financially Independent." Prima Publishing: Roseville, CA.

Clason, George. 2018 (1926). "The Richest Man in Babylon." Sound Wisdom: Shippensburg, PA.

Cothern, Lance. "What is the 50/30/20 rule budget?" *Credit Karma.* Retrieved September 27th, 2020. https://www.creditkarma.com/advice/i/50-30-20-rule

DeMarco, MJ. 2011. "The Millionaire Fastlane: Crack the Code to Wealth and Live Rich for a Lifetime!" Viperion Publishing Corporation: Phoenix.

Duggan, Wayne and John Divine. 2020. "The Complete Berkshire Hathaway Portfolio." *US News.* Retrieved September 27th, 2020. https://money.usnews.com/investing/stock-market-news/slideshows/the-complete-berkshire-hathaway-portfolio?slide=45

Eker, T. Harv. 2005. "Secrets of the Millionaire Mind: Mastering the Inner Game of Wealth." HarperCollins Publishers: New York.

Hills, Napoleon. 2016 (1937). "Think and Grow Rich." The Ralston Society: Meriden, CT.

Kiyosaki, Robert T. 1997. "Rich Dad, Poor Dad: What the Rich Teach Their Kids About Money – That the Poor and Middle Class Do Not!" Warner Books: New York.

Kiyosaki, Robert T. 2011. "Rich Dad's Cashflow Quadrant: Guide to Financial Freedom." Warner Books: New York.

Questrade. Retrieved September 27th, 2020. https://www.questrade.com/home

Robinhood. Retrieved September 27th, 2020. https://robinhood.com/us/en/

Sincero, Jen. 2018. "You Are a Badass at Making Money: Master the Mindset of Wealth." Penguin Books: New York.

The Vanguard Group, Inc. "Don't let high costs eat away your returns." Retrieved September 27th, 2020. https://investor.vanguard.com/investing/how-to-invest/impact-of-costs

US Securities and Exchanges Commission. Office of Investor Education and Advocacy. "How Fees and Expenses

Affect Your Investment Portfolio." *Investor Bulletin.* Retrieved September 27th, 2020. https://www.sec.gov/investor/alerts/ib_fees_expenses.pdf

Wealthsimple. Retrieved September 27th, 2020. https://www.wealthsimple.com/en-us/

Wikipedia. "Compound interest." Retrieved September 27th, 2020. https://en.wikipedia.org/wiki/Compound_interest

Yochim, Dayana and Jonathan Todd. "How a 1% Fee Could Cost Millennials "590,000 in Retirement Savings." *nerdwallet.* Retrieved September 27th, 2020. https://www.nerdwallet.com/blog/investing/millennial-retirement-fees-one-percent-half-million-savings-impact/

Zitter, Leah. 2019. "How Did Ray Dalio Get Rich?" *Investopedia.* Retrieved September 27th, 2020. https://www.investopedia.com/articles/insights/072516/how-did-ray-dalio-get-rich.asp

Fine Margins of Mental Health

Quicker, more effective Strategies That Break Bad Habits and Build Good Ones for All Ages

Sensei Paul David

CONTENTS

FOREWORD 305

CHAPTER ONE   HABITS: WHAT ARE THEY? 311

   Automatic Behaviours Form Half Of Your Waking Activities 312
   Automation Is An Energy-Saving Mechanism Of The Brain 313
   Habits Are Tougher To Break Than Many People Realize 316
   Breaking Habits Involve Spirituality 318

CHAPTER TWO   HABIT OR MENTAL ILLNESS? 321

   Duration Of Habit Formation 321
   Consideration Of The Complexity Of Habit 322
   The 21 Days Myth 323
   The Role Of Context In Habit Formation 324
   Mental Illness Or Bad Habit? 325

CHAPTER THREE   WHY YOU NEED TO BREAK BAD HABITS NOW 331

CHAPTER FOUR   HOW TO LEVERAGE KEYSTONE HABITS 337

   Initiating Positive Changes With Keystone Habits 338
   The Interrelatedness Of Habits 340
   How To Identify Keystone Habits 341
   Implementing Keystone Habits 344

CHAPTER FIVE TECHNIQUES FOR BREAKING BAD HABITS 346

CHAPTER SIX CRUCIAL FACTS TO REMEMBER WHEN BUILDING NEW HABITS 353

CHAPTER SEVEN HOW TO MAINTAIN NEW HABITS 360

The Battle Is Still On 360
Prevent The Triggers Of The Habit 361
Watch Out For Your Relationship 362
Remember Where You Were 363

CHAPTER EIGHT WHEN IT SEEMS YOU ARE LOSING THE PLOT 365

It Is Not Over Until It Is Over 365
It Is Natural To Stumble While Trying To Walk 366
Don't Get Used To It 367
How You Start Does Not Matter 369
Don't Let Guilt Stop You 370
Do More Research 371

INDEX: 373

FOREWORD

Sensei Paul David stands out among the rest when it comes to producing self-help books that have transforming effects. His ability to pay attention to the **fine margins** shines through in this project again. In this book, Paul discusses in detail how you can break limiting habits and build empowering ones.

This project, like his previous works, is full of value, which makes it an engaging book you will not want to put down once you start reading. Paul's ability to help readers convert their curiosity into a beneficial habit for continuous self-education shines through again in this book. This project reflects his training and expertise in this area of life. Besides, his wealth of experience from helping people overcome destructive habits and building beneficial ones, makes him an excellent resource to produce this kind of work.

Most importantly, Paul is a sterling example of a person who has taken advantage of proven techniques to break free from self-destructive behaviours. So, he has what it takes to facilitate structure with a person and lead them through this journey because he has been there before. The content of this book shows that the author is not writing impossible and idealistic works that are not practical in application.

Rather, it is full of simple ideas that can change your life when you practice them. This book is full of fine margins many people ignore, that make tremendous differences when prioritized. Paul has shown once again, with this guide, that the most important things in life are not the sophisticated things but the basic and routine ones many of us ignore, to our detriment.

The truth is that this guide is not a magic wand, in any way, that will suddenly help you break free from addictions and other self-destructive habits. Instead, it gives you the tools and a fighting chance to control your demons. The tips in this material will empower you to make you realize that you can be free from any unhealthy behaviour when you choose to demand your freedom.

It begins by helping you identify what a bad habit is, and carefully takes you through how you can turn the tables. It is full of action plans that will take you from where you are to where you need to be. The best part of your life is about to begin as you pay attention to the fine margins!

Thank You from The Author: Sensei Paul David

Before we dive in, I'd like to thank you for picking up this book. Your time is valuable, and I know there are many other similar books and courses out there that offer to help, but you chose to invest in the mine, and that means everything to me.

Now that you're here, and if you stick with me, I promise to make our time together valuable and worthwhile.

In the pages ahead, you will find some areas of information and practices more helpful than others—and that's great because as you apply what works best, you will benefit from an exciting transformation of character and knowledge. Enjoy!

Welcome

"Most people don't have that willingness to break bad habits. They have a lot of excuses and they talk like victims." **Carlos Santana**

Effective Strategies For Breaking Bad Habits And Building Good Ones

It makes perfect sense to begin this journey by exploring the meaning of the word, "habits."

Habit (noun): a settled tendency or usual manner of behaviour.

In the words of Benjamin Franklin, "It is easier to prevent bad habits than to break them." Indeed, prevention is always better than cure. Nonetheless, it is not all gloom and doom if you have destructive habits you want to let go of. You have started on the right note by having the desire to make the necessary changes to alter the course of your life. This book will provide you with the tools you need to get your life back on track.

Let us explore how you can break limiting habits and build beneficial ones.

Congratulations on starting this and enjoy the process.

Sensei Paul

Chapter One

Habits: What Are They?

Discover Foundational Truths About Habits

Many people assume a lot of different things, including habits. If you are asked to mention bad and good habits, likely, you will not have issues mentioning some of the common ones. Smoking will be at the top of the list of most people, including smokers. It sounds ridiculous that many people who smoke see smoking as a bad habit. Yet, they have not been able to stop themselves from puffing cigarettes and other choice items. This reality shows that there are some things people don't understand about habits that have kept them captive.

I know you are eager to get to that point when we start talking about the steps you can take to break your bad habits and build good ones. However, you will have to be patient. There are some crucial facts about habits you need to understand that will empower you to make lasting changes. If you jump to the tips chapter, you might get some results, but they will be unsustainable.

So, let's ride slowly, but deliberately, to arrive safely at our destination. You cannot change something when you have no idea how it works. This chapter explores vital facts you need to know about habits. Here they are:

AUTOMATIC BEHAVIOURS FORM HALF OF YOUR WAKING ACTIVITIES

You might need to read that again if you think you didn't get it right. It is amazing but it is a reality. I am not framing this up to impress you. It is a fact that is backed up by research.

In 2006, researchers from Duke University carried out a study to investigate how much our brain automates our actions.

Surprisingly, the scientists discovered that up to 45% of our daily behaviours are automated by our brain! It is shocking but that is the truth. This discovery should give you an insight into why it is often difficult to let go of some habits (1).

It is easy to stop doing something when you are consciously doing it. However, it is more challenging to cease to act in certain ways when your brain is in the driver's seat. The logical question anyone will ask after seeing this fact is, "why does the brain act this way?" The answer to this question will lead us to the next fact.

AUTOMATION IS AN ENERGY-SAVING MECHANISM OF THE BRAIN

Your brain forms an insignificant part of your total body mass (2%), but it is the most crucial organ in your body. Once you understand how your brain works, you can break free from any destructive behaviour. Interestingly, the brain consumes 25% of all the oxygen you inhale, which shows how much work it does.

If an organ that consumes that amount of energy is not efficient, it is a complete waste. So, your brain always tries to devise ways of optimizing its use of resources. One of the ways it achieves this is by automating some of your behaviours. It divides a complex pattern into small chunks through automation, which leads to fewer brain activities and energy use.

The human brain is smart enough to recognize when there is no need to spend energy on initiating some complex processes again when it has done them for some time. Your brain recognizes patterns, and when they are similar, it documents them and "replays" them when you find yourself in that situation again.

Results From Animal Studies

Scientists often experiment with animals and extrapolate the results for the benefit of human beings. Due to its similarity with the human brain, the rat brain is often used by researchers. In their bid to understand why and how the brain automates behaviours, they studied brain activities and patterns of rats running through mazes.

In one of the studies, the rats had to find their way through two sections for a piece of chocolate after a clicking noise, which opened the door into the maze.

They did this repeatedly for one week. So, at some point, they realized that all they had to do was turn left to get the chocolate, as soon as the door opened (2).

Their brain had conditioned their bodies to an automatic sequence of response, to reduce the energy expended on processing information while doing the activity. Psychologists call this connection of stimuli and behaviour **Classical Conditioning.** It was first identified by Ivan Pavlov when he noticed the relationship between his dog, the bell, and food.

Pavlov noticed that his dog would salivate after hearing the bell he often rang before serving its food. He realized that it was not so initially. Previously, the dog would only salivate when it saw the food. However, over time, it had come to realize that the bell often rang before the food. So, the dog would salivate when it heard the bell because it had associated the sound with food.

Therapists take advantage of this knowledge to help people break free from addiction, with a therapy known as **aversive conditioning.** It involves associating an unpleasant sensation, such as nausea, with something you do repeatedly, such as smoking.

Habits Are Tougher To Break Than Many People Realize

This fact is not meant to scare you but to make you understand what you are up against. You need to recognize the strength of the enemy to be able to build a defence strong enough to ward off the potential attacks. In the same way, it is vital to understand the reality of what you are trying to overcome, to know the quality of preparation required.

From the last fact about habits, it is obvious that it is not something you can just wake up to one day and change. Indeed, you have to decide when you have had enough. However, sheer determination will not see you through. Understanding how challenging it is to break habits will not only help you with the process, it will also help you to stop being critical of others.

Some people are very judgemental when they see others struggling with an addiction. They will say such things like:

- Doesn't he realize that he is wasting his life?
- Doesn't he realize that life is too short to be wasted on drunkenness?

We are all human, and we need to cut people some slack sometimes. In the words of Kanye West, a popular Hip-Hop artist, "People wouldn't realize you are pushing your buttons, they will say 'type right.' In other words, people don't often realize how hard some people are fighting to overcome their issues but just criticize them for it. If you are going to break free from any damaging behaviour you have had over time, it is crucial to be realistic; it is not a stroll in the park.

The case study of a 71-years old man, Eugene Pauly, suffering from severe memory loss after illness, offers an interesting insight into how hard it can be to break habits. The researchers discovered that habits rooted in the basal ganglia of the brain are so strong that even brain damage cannot destroy them! So, you should not be shocked that you could not quit smoking the day you said you would (3).

BREAKING HABITS INVOLVE SPIRITUALITY

Don't protest yet, especially if you are an atheist or don't have any religious affiliation. Being spiritually conscious does not necessarily mean you attach yourself to a religious sect. It is more about having a belief system, which can be used to your advantage.

Alcoholics Anonymous (AA) is a well-known group boasting close to two million members every year. The society has existed for more than twenty-five years, and it has helped many people, worldwide, recover from alcohol addiction. Indeed, the group has a famous 12-step program. However, you will be making a mistake if you think that their success is based on this formula alone.

The secret to the success of the AA is the belief the organization helps people to build. New members look around and realize that there are other people, like them, that have been able to successfully quit the habit. So, it builds their faith and confidence that they will be able to get rid of their addiction also.

According to research, having any sort of faith makes a huge difference when battling addiction. Indeed, no specific religion can be credited with the success of the AA.

However, the belief shared among the members gives them an advantage over agnostics and atheists (4).

Chapter Two

Habit Or Mental Illness?

You must know the difference between a habit and a mental illness. They are very similar but they differ in some ways. This chapter will explore the differences between the two and how long it takes to form a new habit.

DURATION OF HABIT FORMATION

Various researchers have dug into habit formation and breaking habits and they have discovered some intriguing facts worth noting. Experts believe that it takes an average of 66 days for a new behaviour to become automatic. Ultimately, the breaking of a habit is the formation of a new one. So, usually, the most effective destruction of a bad habit is the formation of a beneficial one to replace it.

There is a consensus among experts of habit formation that it takes between 18 and 254 days to break a habit, depending on its complexity. This agreement was based on the findings of a 2009 study published in the European Journal of Social psychology (5).

CONSIDERATION OF THE COMPLEXITY OF HABIT

The 2009 study is not a one-size-fits-all answer to every habit. Rather, it highlights the differences in the duration of habit formation based on complexity. Some habits take longer to form than others. For example, the study showed that it is more difficult to form a habit of doing 50 sit-ups after morning coffee than drinking a glass of water at breakfast.

The study also explained that some people are more suited than others to form a habit. The result of the research proved that it is not everyone that can be consistent with a routine. Some people will only form a habit that they don't have to perform every day. The spacing of the behaviour makes it more appealing, whenever they do it.

Such people will get tired of having to do something repeatedly and give up on it. However, some people will only be able to form a habit when it is something they do daily, due to one reason or the other.

THE 21 DAYS MYTH

You might have heard people say that it takes 21 days to form a habit. This claim can be traced to a book that was published in 1960 by Dr. Maxwell Maltz. However, unknown to many people, Maltz never claimed that 21 days was what it takes to form a habit. Rather, he was reporting the metric he noticed in his life and his patients during that period (6).

According to him, his observations and other commonly observed phenomena show that it takes 21 days for the dissolution of an old mental image and the gelling of a new one. Nonetheless, since over thirty million copies of the book were sold, it is not strange that the observation became a widely accepted fact.

THE ROLE OF CONTEXT IN HABIT FORMATION

Habits are actions that are triggered automatically as responses to contextual cues that have been associated with their performance, according to a study published in the British Journal of General Practice, in 2012. This study showed that certain concepts prompt some specific behaviour (7).

For example, you automatically put on your seat belt when you get into your car. Your brain does not take time to process the action because the context prompted the activation of a documented pattern. As discussed earlier, your brain likes these habits because they help it to save energy.

Habits that provide pleasure are the most difficult to break. They get stronger when they offer instant gratification. Indeed, they may cause long-term health challenges. Nonetheless, the fact that the person will derive immediate pleasure from the action makes people repeat them all the same.

A study carried out by the National Institute of Health (NIH) found that habits that are pleasure-based make the brain release dopamine. Dopamine is a hormone that induces a pleasant feeling. So, people will want to repeat a behaviour that leads to its release (8).

Your brain recognizes the contexts that lead to the release of this hormone. It is the reason you are already feeling good before you eat your favourite meal or meet a woman or man you admire. The release of this hormone is one of the reasons people struggle with habits that ruin their health and relationships.

MENTAL ILLNESS OR BAD HABIT?

In this last section of this chapter, let's narrow down the ways you can tell the difference between a psychological problem and a bad habit. You must know the difference because they don't require the same solutions. Bad habits are more under your control. So, you can find it easier to break them.

However, when you are battling mental illness, it becomes more complex and complicated to overcome it. In most cases, you will have to see a therapist before you can be free from such behaviours. Below are some bad habits and similar psychological issues:

Bad Memory Versus Face Blindness

I am sure that you have met many young people who struggle to remember some things. Some people also find it difficult to remember the face of a person unless they have seen that person a couple of times. So, it is normal that you find yourself failing to recognize a person's face sometimes.

Besides, research has proven that the ability to remember facial features depends on age and brain development. Your brain is at its peak when it comes to facial recognition between the ages of 30 and 34. Nonetheless, some might be suffering from a mental illness called Prosopagnosia or face blindness (9).

People suffering from this disorder struggle to recognize the faces of their acquaintances. Such people have alternative ways of recognizing people such as by their voice and hairdo. If anyone they know changes the way they speak, such individuals will not be able to recognize them.

Neatness Consciousness Versus OCD

You might have met people that are so conscious about their environment's cleanliness that it annoys you. There is nothing wrong with being neat because personal hygiene gives you a higher chance of staying healthy. Besides, tidiness is good for your mental health.

Nonetheless, some might be battling Obsessive-Compulsive Disorder when you are cleaning or performing any other repetitive action. Such individuals have a constant desire to get rid of obsessive involuntary thoughts and ideas. When they get scared because they haven't cleaned their home, some might need to talk to a therapist for diagnosis.

Whining Versus Hypochondria

Some people have a bad habit of whining or complaining to attract attention to themselves. Such a person will also manipulate others by making them feel that they are responsible for their problems. It can be extremely difficult to cope with such people, especially when you are married to them.

Nevertheless, it can be more than a simple case of whining sometimes. In some cases, the person might be battling hypochondria. This psychological problem is manifested by constant worry about falling ill. Even when such a person does not feel sick, he or she will still be searching for symptoms.

Greed Versus Syllogomania

We all have a natural tendency to be selfish. So, the fact that you don't like sharing your belongings with others does not mean that you have a psychological problem. Some might just be greedy and need to get rid of that bad habit as soon as possible.

Nonetheless, some might be struggling with a mental illness, called Syllogomania or pathological hoarding. It is a psychological problem when you have so many belongings in your space that it prevents you from living a normal life.

Absent-Mindedness Versus Topographical Disorientation

You are not alone if you sometimes get lost in your hometown. You don't need to see a psychologist yet. Likely, you are only bad at spatial thinking. Many people have this issue and it is sometimes inherited.

However, you should be concerned when you sometimes get lost in your own house. It is ridiculous when you start finding it difficult to locate your kitchen! At that stage, it is in your best interest to consider a psychological examination. You might be suffering from topographical disorientation.

Bad Mood Versus Depression

We all feel bad sometimes, due to unpleasant situations that are part and parcel of life. When some people are not happy, they say they are depressed. However, depression is far more severe than being in a bad mood. The fact that you are sad does not mean that you are battling depression.

Depression is a psychological problem that is often characterized by consistent negative emotions and social withdrawal. Depressed people find it impossible to derive pleasure from situations and things that usually make other people happy. You might need the help of an expert to get out of that pit before things get worse.

Chapter Three

Why You Need To Break Bad Habits Now

Breaking bad habits improves your life in many ways that you may never realize until you have done it. In this chapter, we will explore the benefits you stand to enjoy when you break some bad habits. This section aims to give you more reasons and impetus to destroy limiting behaviours.

Improved Memory

Indeed, quitting smoking has numerous health benefits. Besides, it can also improve your relationship with the people in your life. However, researchers have found that you can improve the efficiency of your memory when you let go of this bad habit. Scientists at Northumbria University studied the effects of smoking on the brain (10).

They discovered that people who smoke are in danger of losing one-third of their everyday memory. The research showed that smokers performed much worse than non-smokers when they were required to carry out memory tasks. Interestingly, these researchers also discovered that quitting smoking restores the ability to recollect information.

Enhanced Smartness

You might have heard that too much sugar is bad for your health because it increases your chance of getting diabetes. It is true. However, excessive sugar might also be responsible for your inability to think clearly. A study by researchers at the University of California, Los Angeles, has proven this.

During the research, some rats were fed a diet containing high-fructose corn syrup. Due to that, they struggled to find their way through a maze. Meanwhile, they had mastered how to navigate their way through the maze before then. So, it was obvious that excessive sugar disrupted their ability to think clearly (11).

Longer Lifespan

You might find it shocking but researchers have discovered that you could shorten your lifespan by watching too much television. Scientists at the University of Queensland discovered that you can lose as much as 22 minutes every time you spend one-hour watching television (11).

I am sure that you don't want to do the math for how much you shorten your lifespan by when you have a habit of watching movies for over six hours daily within ten years. Indeed, total abstinence might not be feasible. However, you can reduce the time you spend watching television to increase your chances of increasing your lifespan.

Fewer Wrinkles

Many people look older than their real ages in the modern world. You might be doing your best to ensure that you look younger and avoid premature ageing. However, you might be getting more wrinkles due to your sweet tooth.

Research has shown that excess consumption of tasty sweet treats causes wrinkles to appear on the skin. Other causes include exposure to sunlight and also smoking. According to scientists, high blood sugar levels lead to glycation, which hardens the collagen in the skin and leads to wrinkles. Therefore, reducing sugar intake can improve your appearance.

Reduction Of The Risk Of Dementia

Dementia is common among the elderly. However, you are at risk of battling this health condition when you have the habit of getting worried or anger issues. The link between negative emotions and brain health was discovered by researchers at Rush University Medical Center, in Chicago (12).

The study discovered that people who have negative emotions, such as worry and anger, are at greater risk of dementia. The researchers suggest that such people should embrace relaxation techniques or counselling. So, by breaking the bad habit of anxiety and being bad-tempered, you can reduce the risk of battling dementia.

Enhanced Financial Stability

The primary way of becoming financially stable and independent is by earning money by offering goods and services to people. However, you can increase your chances of not going bankrupt by avoiding some habits, such as excessive alcohol consumption.

Alcohol consumption does not only affect your health; it also affects your finances. The money spent on alcohol could have been utilized in more useful endeavours. So, think about the financial implications of the habit. It could give you the motivation needed to quit.

Improved Mood

It is not unlikely that you wish you could drink a magic potion that would keep you happy for the rest of your life. Sadly, such a substance does not exist. You have to be motivated and driven to live a happy life. One of the ways you can improve your mood is by ditching junk food.

According to a study published in the Public Health Nutrition Journal, people who eat fast foods regularly, are more likely to develop depression than those who don't (13). So, think twice next time before you tuck into that greasy kebab or pizza.

Chapter Four

How To Leverage Keystone Habits

In a football team, there are certain footballers known as "key players." Although soccer is a team sport where every player has to play a vital role, key players are difference makers. When they perform well, it covers the lapses of others in the team. They often make others elevate their games and perform better when they are in full flow.

In the same way, it is best to be able to recognize keystone habits to increase your chances of breaking a bad habit. In the book, *The Power of Habit* Charles Duhigg describes particular types of habits as **Keystone Habits**. What are these? These are habits or changes that people introduce into their daily routines that have ripple effects on other behaviours.

In other words, changing these habits will empower you to change other limiting behaviours you have always wanted to get rid of in your life. In most cases, the impact of these habits is automated. Once you change them, you will realize that you are also letting go of other unhealthy behaviours you used to have. This chapter will explore how you can identify and leverage keystone habits to improve your life.

INITIATING POSITIVE CHANGES WITH KEYSTONE HABITS

Positive changes begin with keystone habits. Smoking and excessive alcohol consumption are some of the most common habits people want to change. However, in the "habit hole," there are many things you want to change. However, you might not prioritize them because they don't have obvious effects on you, like smoking and excessive alcohol consumption.

Other behaviours you might want to quit include eating too much, procrastination, and irregular exercise. Once you recognize a keystone habit and change it, others will fall into place. The story of Paul O'Neill, former CEO of Alcoa, a huge aluminum company, is a fantastic example of the success a person can attain when he or she recognizes and takes advantage of, keystone habits.

When he became the CEO of the organization in 1987, he started his first speech by saying that he wanted to talk about worker safety. Many investors and stakeholders were disappointed in him because they didn't expect something that "lame." Some of them called their clients to inform them that the company had appointed a crazy hippie that would ruin the company.

However, he had the last laugh eventually. By the time he retired, in 2000, he had multiplied the company's income by fivefold, simply by ensuring that no worker stapled their foot to the ground! O'Neill had found that one of the key reasons the company was losing money was because workers were injuring themselves.

So, by ensuring workers' safety, he was able to help the company save more and earn more profits than his predecessors. His legacy remains until today. Over 80 percent of the company's locations did not lose any workers due to injuries in 2010.

You don't have to start big. Nonetheless, like O'Neill, choose the right habit. It is just like when Indy had to select the right cup in *The Last Crusade*.

THE INTERRELATEDNESS OF HABITS

We will continue to explore keystone habits by focusing on the interrelated nature of behaviours. According to Duhigg, some habits are connected. Once you have one, you will likely have the other. For example, kids who grow up in families where they eat together are likely to be more confident and have higher self-esteem.

The ripple effect of high self-esteem is good grades. In the same way, people who don't struggle to make their beds daily are not likely to have issues with regular exercise. Also, planning your week will inspire you to want to get into productive activities. Therefore, you have an edge over people that just go into the week without a plan.

These links do not mean that one habit directly produces the other. Rather, it shows that one action makes it likely for you to produce the other. According to Duhigg, the positive ripple effect is not usually deliberate. Nonetheless, there is no crime in choosing to be deliberate about incorporating some more habits after starting one.

How To Identify Keystone Habits

Note that keystone habits are not universal to everyone. So, it is in your best interest to find what works best for you. Once you discover them, always ensure that they win whenever you are considering the impact and influences of the changes you are making.

To identify keystone habits, it is vital to recognize the habits that have the **highest impact and influence** on you. For example, exercise is a keystone habit because it affects many other things you do during the day. After you workout in the morning, you will feel good, but it does not end there.

It also makes you more focused during the day, which ensures that you make fewer mistakes. Fewer mistakes will make you more effective, which ensures that you will be in a good mood because you are happy with your performance. Meanwhile, good performances can earn you commendations and promotion at work.

Exercise will not directly lead to commendation and promotion at work. However, it can be a positive ripple effect that eventually leads there. Besides, you might have been drinking heavily because you are not happy with yourself. Regular exercise might be the keystone habit that will improve your mood and make you realize that you don't need alcohol to feel better.

Other habits have carryover effects on other aspects of your life. Getting quality sleep is another keystone habit that can be highly impactful. When you sleep well, you will be more relaxed and energized for the activities of the next day. It will ensure that you don't doze off during work hours, which ensures you avoid issues with your boss.

Meanwhile, avoiding issues with your boss and being effective at work will increase your chances of being successful and having good moods. So, it is not likely you abuse substances to relax when you have a habit of enjoying restorative sleep. Read *Restoring Restorative Rest* by the same author for more information on how you can make your bedroom a sanctuary.

Implementing Keystone Habits

The mistake many people make when making changes in their lives is that they have too many they want to change at once. This error in judgment is one of the reasons many people find themselves failing after planning to quit some bad habits they have.

It is commendable that you are eager to make positive changes in your life. Nevertheless, it will be counterproductive if you are in a hurry. Begin by choosing a particular habit before moving on to the next one. For example, you might choose to start with your irregular sleep pattern.

The first habit you will need in that regard is to make your bed early. Making your bed early can be that perfect tonic that will encourage you to go to sleep on time. Usually, when your bed is disorganized, you might want to stay up to do other things until you get exhausted and have no choice but to sleep.

Meanwhile, when you sleep because you are exhausted, it is not likely you wake up energized. It is on such days that you wake up feeling lazy and tired. After you have fixed your sleeping habit, move on to the next one. Your success in the previous one will buoy you to make future changes.

You can also apply this same principle when leading a group. Identify the keystone habits that can have positive ripple effects on your team members rather than try to change multiple habits. O'Neil was able to do that, and the rest is history.

Chapter Five

Techniques For Breaking Bad Habits

Anyone can choose to break free from a bad habit. However, it takes more than deciding to break a bad habit. If you want to follow through with your decision, it is in your best interest to be informed. It is crucial to learn effective techniques that can make your dream a reality. This chapter will explore these strategies.

Be Determined To Stop

Breaking a bad habit goes beyond being resolute to overcome it. Nonetheless, you may want to start by making up your mind to turn things around. It is determination that will make you find the techniques that will enable you to be effective on the journey.

Most likely, you picked up this book because you are determined to make positive changes in your life that will improve its quality. Therefore, you are on the right path to freedom. Your determination will give you the motivation and momentum needed to follow through with your plan.

Be Realistic

If you have more than one habit you want to tackle, you have to be realistic about your expectations. It is not feasible to overcome multiple habits at once unless they are very similar. So, don't get too emotional about your new journey.

It is always the best approach to pick one habit at a time. You cannot stop drinking, quit smoking, and stop consuming chocolate all in one week. Start by thinking about the simplest between the habits. When you identify it, begin with it. Your victory over the first one will inspire you when tackling the harder ones.

Take It One Day At A Time

You mustn't make decisions based on how you feel at that point. Sometimes, people vow never to do something again because it cost them big at some point. Due to the feeling of guilt, such people will vow never to do that thing ever again.

In most cases, they end up going back to their "vomit" again. To increase your chances of breaking a habit, take it one day at a time. In other words, plan to avoid the behaviour for that day only. Days will become weeks, and weeks will become months. Before you know it, you are free from the habit for years.

Speak To Someone You Trust And Respect

You can "set up" yourself to stick with your plan to stop a habit by being open about it. The best way to do this is by speaking to someone that can question your actions. It becomes more challenging when you are not the only person aware of your decision to quit a craving.

However, when you know that someone would ask you about your progress, you will be more careful. Another way you can ensure you keep your commitment is by documenting your progress in an online blog. You will be more resilient because you want to impress your "followers." So, it will increase your chances of quitting the habit for good.

Find A Partner

Competition often pushes us to perform better, in most cases. You can take advantage of that reality when trying to break a habit. Find a person that is also trying to break the same habit. It is essential that the person also wants to overcome the habit at the same time as you.

You and the other person can push yourselves by discussing your progress. Naturally, you will not want the other person to do better than you. Due to this, you will want to ensure that you don't default. You will also be able to share tips that can help the other person when you discover that one of you is doing better than the other.

Eliminate Temptation

Your effort to stay free from a habit will be futile when you fail to remove the things that can stir up the craving. For example, if you are trying to overcome the urge to watch pornographic content, you have to avoid visiting sites that have suggestive images.

In the same way, it's best to empty your house of cigarettes, alcohol, treats, or whatever you want to avoid. You will increase your chances of avoiding such things when you don't see them at all.

Change Your Friends

It is very difficult to do things your friends don't do. You will not want to feel like an outcast, and that will make you conform to the habits of your inner circle. So, one of the best decisions you can make when breaking a habit is to stay away from the people who have that habit.

You can inform them first that you don't want to live your life that way any longer. They may support you and plan to join you on your new journey to liberation. However, you will have to leave that association when they mock you and discourage you.

Set Regular Habit Reminders

Habits are so powerful that you can perform them unconsciously, sometimes. So, it is in your best interest to do all you can to ensure that you don't find yourself doing something you don't want to do. One of the ways you can be on guard is by setting habit reminders.

You can use your phone to remind yourself not to eat junk food that day. At some point in my life, I had to set a reminder not to call someone that often ruined my mood. You mustn't overestimate yourself. You don't have to keep regretting your actions. Instead, you can ensure you don't do the wrong things.

Chapter Six

Crucial Facts To Remember When Building New Habits

Breaking bad habits is not enough. If you are going to sustain the decision, you have to build new healthy ones. Some essential facts are crucial to know, that will help you develop new beneficial habits. This chapter highlights them.

Building New Habits Is Not Optional

Developing new habits is not something you can choose to do or not. You will fall back into the old ditch when you don't replace the old habits with new ones. If you used to consume excess sugar, it is best to think about something else you can consume instead.

In the same way, if you used to spend a lot of time with your digital devices, it is in your best interest to think about something else to do with the time. For example, you might choose to spend more time with your friends and family. Humans are not designed to be inactive unless they are asleep. It is vital to find something constructive you can be doing with your time.

Ensure You Have A Sense Of Purpose

One of the ways you can stay away from your old habits is to ensure that the new ones give you a sense of purpose. For example, instead of hanging out with friends who drink, you can choose to join a club or reach out to an orphanage.

If you find purpose and meaning by helping such people, it becomes more difficult for you to go back to your old friends and habits. You will be glad that you are contributing to the lives of others and that gives you enough of a "high" instead of falling back to smoking or drinking.

Make It Fun

You should take your time before choosing a habit that can replace an unhealthy one. If you choose something that you will not find exciting, it is likely you revert to your "default mode." The reason you spend a lot of time playing games or watching television is that it is interesting.

So, you must find something that can still give you that feeling without hurting you. Getting involved in a sport is your best bet in this regard. You will look forward to doing it all over again, especially when you gain the skills to excel in it.

Avoid The Bandwagon

The desire to be accepted is entrenched in human nature. We all want to do things that will make others acknowledge us. However, you have to be careful to avoid doing things just because they are popular. Rather, you should be convinced that you are doing the right thing.

Why do you want to lose weight? Is it because it is in vogue or because you want to improve your physique? If you want to stop eating some things because everyone else wants to look slim, you will end up reverting to the previous habit when it is no longer a popular choice.

According to a Chicago-based psychological performance coach and the author of *Chasing Success,* Alok Trivedi, when you set goals based on the values of others, you will end up frustrated, resentful, and disappointed.

Find A Coach

There are always people that are more knowledgeable and experienced than you in every area of your life. Such people can offer you "shortcuts" that will make your journey smoother and faster. You can hire such a person when you are trying to break a habit.

You will be accountable to that person, and he or she will be able to provide you with helpful tips that can help you succeed in your bid to get rid of a limiting habit. According to the owner of TS Fitness in New York City, Naom Tamir, a coach will connect with you and motivate you to ensure that you don't drop the ball.

Leverage Positive Affirmations

You cannot underestimate the value of your words in whatever you are doing. Your affirmations can set you on your way to success or quench the zeal to move forward. So, your affirmations are part of you to fight your addictions and build healthy habits.

If you keep saying that you cannot sustain your new habits, you will end up reverting to the old ones. Naturally, thoughts of defeat might run through your mind. However, you mustn't speak them out loud. Instead, put your mind in order by speaking words that will encourage you to stay on course.

A study published in the Journal of Personality and Social Psychology Bulletin showed that people perform better when they employ self-affirmations. Besides, speaking positive words makes you calmer (16).

Always Remember Why You Are Doing It

You are like a sailor directing a ship when forming new habits; you cannot afford to lose sight of the reason you are on the journey. When you lose sight of the purpose of your new commitment, you will not be motivated to continue doing it.

Be Consistent

Most of your daily activities are performed each day in almost the same situation, according to a study in the Society for Personality and Social Psychology. This research shows that repetition is key to forming a habit. So, just like the unhealthy ones, you have to be consistent in strengthening beneficial ones.

Keep doing it and remind yourself about the reason you are doing the activity, to keep you focused. Once you are consistent, you will end up keeping your old demons away for good.

Find People With Similar Habits

In the same way, your old habits were fuelled by friends, you also need a new association that can help you sustain the new habit. According to psychologists, role models are crucial in helping us develop new habits. When you have people who have similar behaviours, it becomes easier to act that way.

We were made to live in a community. Plato framed it exquisitely when he said, "Anyone who thrives in isolation is either a beast or a deity." Regardless of your choice in life, it is essential to find a community where you can grow. You need people who share your worldview to feel accepted and loved.

It is in your best interest not to compromise your standards just for acceptance. However, there is no doubt that we all want to be in a place where we feel that we belong. Even an outcast needs a group of outcasts in which to thrive.

Chapter Seven

How To Maintain New Habits

There is no point in breaking a habit when you will end up picking it up again later. The success of anything is not the fact that it happened but because it is sustainable. Therefore, you must understand what you need to do to ensure that you retain your new habit. This chapter will discuss how you can retain the new beneficial habits you form after breaking limiting ones.

THE BATTLE IS STILL ON

Due to the proliferation of various social media platforms, such as Facebook, Instagram, and Twitter, many people have endless opportunities to share their experiences with others. Therefore, many people take advantage of these sites to post their improvements in various aspects of their lives.

Some people would post about the changes in their weight after going through a weight loss program. Also, some people would post about their newly developed abs after working out for a while. So, it is not surprising that you share your excitement with your friends and family after you quit smoking or excessive alcohol consumption for some weeks.

However, it is recommended that you not be too excited. The same triggers that made you pick up the habit in the first place, can still make you fall into it all over again. So, you mustn't become a victim of your success. People will feel you are a hypocrite or a deceiver when they find you doing the things you claimed you had stopped doing.

PREVENT THE TRIGGERS OF THE HABIT

Every habit has a trigger. You might start consuming a lot of alcohol whenever you remember what your previous spouse did to you. In the same way, you might start eating unhealthily whenever you are stressed. So, you must avoid the triggers as much as possible so that you will not find yourself in the same spot again.

In the case of stress, you have to plan your day so that you will be able to have time for every crucial thing you need to do. Indeed, you cannot always predict the day because there might be unforeseen circumstances that might ruin your plans. However, you stand a better chance to have a good day when you have a clear plan for it.

It is crucial to also explore ways you can relieve stress, without resorting to food. There are countless articles and posts online that can help you in this regard. Read them to know different techniques you can use to manage stress effectively to improve the quality of your life.

WATCH OUT FOR YOUR RELATIONSHIP

Many people were never promiscuous until they met that friend who made them feel that it was alright to sleep with multiple partners. Whoever you surround yourself with, you will eventually become. They might be resistant to the strange idea initially, but they will end up succumbing over time.

Parents understand the effect of their kids being surrounded by the right people, and that is why they are often wary of the influence around their children. If you are to succeed in remaining astute in sticking to your new habit, it is vital to surround yourself with people who will help you keep your focus.

REMEMBER WHERE YOU WERE

A quick reminder of what you stand to lose by going back to your "vomit", can be good enough to help you keep your focus. I am sure you don't want to go back to your former out-of-sorts physique, health problems, discrimination, and being targets of cyberbullies.

You cannot afford to lose your momentum. Your new habits are making you healthier and improving your relationships. So, why should you lose all of that just because of instant gratification? It doesn't make sense in any way, and that is why you have to stick to your new habits.

Chapter Eight

When It Seems You Are Losing The Plot

A recurrent theme you would have noticed all through this book is that **habits are not easy to break**. It is easier to form them than to destroy them because the brain loves them. They help the brain save a lot of energy, which makes it difficult to reverse the documented patterns.

Therefore, it should not be surprising to you that you stumble on your way to breaking free from addiction. In this last chapter, we will explore crucial tips that will help you keep fighting when it looks as though you are losing the battle.

IT IS NOT OVER UNTIL IT IS OVER

This is the rallying call you need during those days when it seems you will never be able to break free from a habit. You had made up your mind not to eat food again to relieve your stress. However, here you are doing it again. Naturally, you feel bad about yourself. You should. Nonetheless, you cannot afford to give up on yourself at this point.

Those periods are the best times to read stories of people who were able to break free from addictions. As long as you keep fighting, you have a chance. You can still be free from the entanglement of smoking or any other habit you desire to drop, as long as you don't throw in the towel.

IT IS NATURAL TO STUMBLE WHILE TRYING TO WALK

Before babies begin to run, they crawl, then walk. It will be ridiculous for anyone to laugh at a baby because he is stumbling while trying to take his first few steps. Everyone knows that it is natural for a child to fall at different points before he or she can have a solid footing.

Picture your struggles with a habit as the crawling stage and your efforts to break free as the walking stage. See the days you slip back into the bad habit as a stumbling period. You mustn't see it as the end of it all. Just like a baby, you have to try again.

Yes, you didn't do well yesterday. You did it all over again. You feel ashamed and disappointed. Hey! You only stumbled! You can still rise up and walk again. The only person that can decide whether you can continue is you. Even if no one is giving you a chance, you have to back yourself to get through this.

DON'T GET USED TO IT

When people struggle with a disease for a long period, they often make an identity out of it. Some individuals will tell their friends during conversations, "you know my issue …" The statements seem harmless on the surface because they have been battling the medical condition for a while.

Nevertheless, you mustn't make a profile out of whatever it is you are trying to overcome. The addiction does not belong to you. Rather, it was a habit you picked up and you are looking for a way to drop it from your life.

You must never get used to it. You must keep seeing it as something that you have to get rid of as soon as possible. When you start making an identity out of a habit you are trying to break, you are already resigning yourself to failure, even though you might not admit it.

That mental state will make you psychologically weak and incapable of producing the willpower you will need to overcome the habit. Nothing can take the place of determination when battling a habit, even though you need more than just that. Nonetheless, as long as you retain the willpower to improve, you are in with a fighting chance.

How You Start Does Not Matter

The advantage of a good start in anything in life is that it gives you the platform to build momentum and reach the finish line on time. However, a good start does not guarantee that you will succeed in the long run. Therefore, it is not the beginning that matters but what you do after starting.

If you have started well in the first few days, congratulations to you. However, the real battle is about to start. Will you be able to resist the urge to puff another cigarette when you see your friends doing the same? Many people admit that they get the best opportunities to do something after they have determined not to do it again.

It is usually when you have decided to lose weight that your friends are inviting you to different parties with mouth-watering dishes. If care is not taken, you can lose your focus and eat as much as you want on those occasions.

So, don't be carried away by your commendable start. You have to keep striving to maintain the quality standard you have set. On the contrary, if you have had a false start, that is not the end of the story. You can still dust yourself off, get up and try to do better next time. It is vital to never forget that it is not about the start but how you end, that matters.

DON'T LET GUILT STOP YOU

One of the greatest impediments to breaking a habit is guilt. It is logical to feel bad when you are not doing what you are supposed to do. However, you have to let go of the negative feelings as fast as possible. If you dwell too much on your mistakes, you will give up on yourself eventually.

You might end up convincing yourself that you don't have the discipline to overcome the habit and then continue to indulge in it. So, be quick to forgive yourself on those days when you fall short of the standard you have set for yourself. If necessary, speak to a person that can encourage you to start the journey again.

You will be making a mistake if you choose to speak to a person that is also struggling with the habit. Such a person likely makes you feel that you are unnecessarily being hard on yourself. So, it matters who you talk to during your low moments.

DO MORE RESEARCH

Sometimes, the reason you are not getting the desired results is not that you are not trying hard enough but because you lack the information to do it properly. So, you must keep finding out whether you are using the right technique that will enhance your effectiveness.

For example, if you are trying to get more quality sleep, it is vital to avoid the consumption of substances like alcohol and caffeine, especially close to your sleep time. Consuming such substances will only make your effort to sleep early, futile.

In the same way, you have to be open to learning to understand potential red flags on your journey to overcome a habit. Once you can identify the factors that can waste your effort, you are a step closer to freedom. So, never stop educating yourself because the quality of your life depends on your exposure to relevant information.

Index:

1. Neal, David & Wood, Wendy & Quinn, Jeffrey. (2006). Habits—A Repeat Performance. Current Directions in Psychological Science - CURR DIRECTIONS PSYCHOL SCI. 15. 198-202. 10.1111/j.1467-8721.2006.00435.x.

2. Smith, K. S., & Graybiel, A. M. (2014). Investigating habits: strategies, technologies and models. *Frontiers in behavioural neuroscience*, 8, 39. https://doi.org/10.3389/fnbeh.2014.00039

3. Stefanacci, Lisa & Buffalo, Elizabeth & Schmolck, Heike & Squire, Larry. (2000). Profound Amnesia After Damage to the Medial Temporal Lobe: A Neuroanatomical and Neuropsychological Profile of Patient E. P. The Journal of neuroscience: the official journal of the Society for Neuroscience. 20.

7024-36. 10.1523/JNEUROSCI.20-18-07024.2000.

4. Grim, B. J., & Grim, M. E. (2019). Belief, Behavior, and Belonging: How Faith is Indispensable in Preventing and Recovering from Substance Abuse. *Journal of religion and health*, *58*(5), 1713–1750. https://doi.org/10.1007/s10943-019-00876-w

5. Lally, Phillippa & Jaarsveld, Cornelia & Potts, Henry & Wardle, Jane. (2010). How are habits formed: Modeling habit formation in the real world. *European Journal of Social Psychology*. 40. 10.1002/ejsp.674.

6. Stawarz, K., Gardner, B., Cox, A., & Blandford, A. (2020). What influences the selection of contextual cues when starting a new routine behaviour? An exploratory study. *BMC psychology*, *8*(1), 29. https://doi.org/10.1186/s40359-020-0394-9

7. Substance Abuse and Mental Health Services Administration (US); Office of the Surgeon General (US). Facing Addiction in America: The Surgeon General's Report on Alcohol, Drugs, and Health [Internet]. Washington (DC): US Department of Health and Human Services; 2016 Nov. CHAPTER 2, THE NEUROBIOLOGY OF SUBSTANCE USE, MISUSE, AND ADDICTION. Available from: https://www.ncbi.nlm.nih.gov/books/NBK424849/

8. Tsao, D. Y., & Livingstone, M. S. (2008). Mechanisms of face perception. *Annual review of neuroscience*, 31, 411–437. https://doi.org/10.1146/annurev.neuro.30.051606.094238

9. Xu, J., Mendrek, A., Cohen, M. S., Monterosso, J., Simon, S., Brody, A. L., Jarvik, M., Rodriguez, P., Ernst, M., & London, E. D. (2006). Effects of acute smoking on brain activity vary with abstinence in smokers performing the N-

Back task: a preliminary study. *Psychiatry Research*, *148*(2-3), 103–109. https://doi.org/10.1016/j.pscychresns.2006.09.005

10. Tryon, M. S., Stanhope, K. L., Epel, E. S., Mason, A. E., Brown, R., Medici, V., Havel, P. J., & Laugero, K. D. (2015). Excessive Sugar Consumption May Be a Difficult Habit to Break: A View From the Brain and Body. *The Journal of clinical endocrinology and metabolism*, *100*(6), 2239–2247. https://doi.org/10.1210/jc.2014-4353

11. Toop, C. R., & Gentili, S. (2016). Fructose Beverage Consumption Induces a Metabolic Syndrome Phenotype in the Rat: A Systematic Review and Meta-Analysis. *Nutrients*, *8*(9), 577. https://doi.org/10.3390/nu809057

12. Guzmán-Vélez, E., Feinstein, J. S., & Tranel, D. (2014). Feelings without memory in Alzheimer's disease. *Cognitive and*

behavioural neurology : official journal of the Society for Behavioral and Cognitive Neurology, 27(3), 117–129. https://doi.org/10.1097/WNN.0000000000000020

13. Ljungberg, T., Bondza, E., & Lethin, C. (2020). Evidence of the Importance of Dietary Habits Regarding Depressive Symptoms and Depression. *International journal of environmental research and public health*, 17(5), 1616. https://doi.org/10.3390/ijerph17051616

Thank you for reading this book!

If you found this book helpful, I would be grateful if you would post an honest review on Amazon so this book can reach and help other people.

All you need to do is to visit amazon.com/author/senseipauldavid click the correct book cover, and click on the blue link next to the yellow stars that says, "customer reviews."

As always...
It's a great day to be alive!

Check Out Another Book in This Series Visit:

www.amazon.com/author/senseipauldavid

Or

Search Amazon.com #senseipublishing

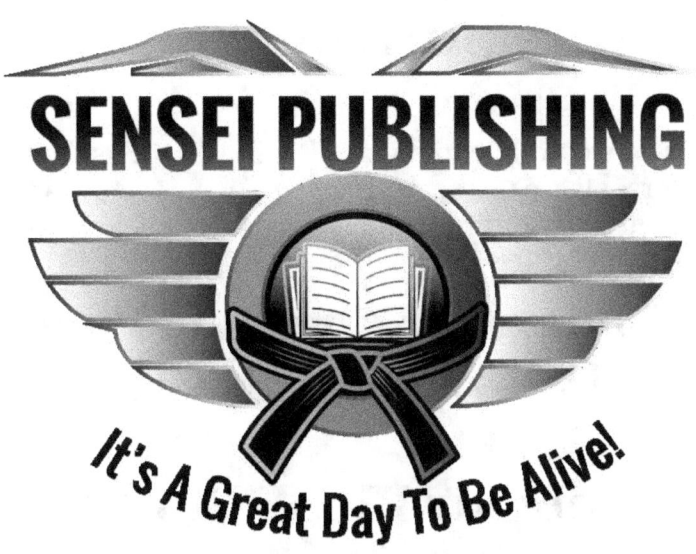

www.senseipublishing.com

@senseipublishing
#senseipublishing

Check out our **recommendations** for other books for adults & kids plus other great resources by visiting
www.senseipublishing.com/resources/

Join Our Publishing Journey!

If you would like to receive FREE BOOKS, special offers, please visit www.senseipublishing.com and join our newsletter by entering your email address in the pop-up box

Follow Our Engaging Blog NOW! senseipauldavid.ca

Get Our FREE Books Today!

Click & Share the Links Below

FREE Kids Books
lifeofbailey.senseipublishing.com
kidsonearth.senseipublishing.com

FREE Self-Development Book
senseiselfdevelopment.senseipublishing.com

FREE BONUS!!!
Experience Over 25 FREE Engaging Guided Meditations!

Prized Skills & Practices for Adults & Kids. Help Restore Deep-Sleep, Lower Stress, Improve Posture, Navigate Uncertainty & More.

Download the Free Insight Timer App and click the link below:
http://insig.ht/sensei_paul

If you like these meditations & want to go deeper email me for a FREE 30min LIVE Coaching Session:
senseipauldavid@senseipublishing.com

About Sensei Publishing

Sensei Publishing commits itself to help people of all ages transform into better versions of themselves by providing high-quality and research-based self-development books with an emphasis on mental health and guided meditations. Sensei Publishing offers well-written e-books, audiobooks, paperbacks and online courses that simplify complicated but practical topics in line with its mission to inspire people towards positive transformation.

It's a great day to be alive!

About the Author

I create simple & transformative eBooks & Guided Meditations for Adults & Children proven to help navigate uncertainty, solve niche problems & bring families closer together.

I'm a former finance project manager, private pilot, jiu-jitsu instructor, musician & former University of Toronto Fitness Trainer. I prefer a science-based approach to focus on these & other areas in my life to stay humble & hungry to evolve. I hope you enjoy my work and I'd love to hear your feedback.

- It's a great day to be alive!
Sensei Paul David

Scan & Follow/Like/Subscribe:
Facebook, Instagram, YouTube:
@senseipublishing

Scan using your phone/iPad camera for Social Media

Visit us at www.senseipublishing.com and sign up to our newsletter to learn more about our exciting books and to experience our FREE Guided Meditations for Kids & Adults.

www.ingramcontent.com/pod-product-compliance
Lightning Source LLC
Chambersburg PA
CBHW071426070526
44578CB00001B/14